HAPPY CHRISTMAS

GOD BLESS THE MASTER

God bless the master of this house,
    The mistress also,
And all the little children
    That round the table go:

And all your kin and kinsfolk
    That dwell both far and near;
We wish you a merry Christmas,
    And a happy New Year.

Anon

HAPPY CHRISTMAS

compiled by

William Kean Seymour and John Smith

illustrated by

Beryl Sanders

BURKE LONDON

222 69700 8

Burke Publishing Company Limited,
14 John Street, London, W.C.1.

Printed by William Clowes & Sons Ltd.,
Beccles, Suffolk.

ACKNOWLEDGEMENTS

Thanks are due to the following poets, authors, agents and publishers for permission to reprint copyright works in this anthology.

Permission for further publication or performance should be sought from these copyright-holders.

A. D. Peters & Co., for *Mrs. Markham on Christmas* from *Mrs. Markham's New History of England* by Hilaire Belloc

John Murray Ltd., for *Christmas* from *Collected Poems* by John Betjeman

Wm. Collins Sons & Co., Ltd., for *Paddington's Christmas* from *More About Paddington* by Michael Bond

Charles Causley and Rupert Hart-Davis Ltd., for *Sailor's Carol* from *Union Street* by Charles Causley

Miss D. E. Collins and J. M. Dent & Sons Ltd., for *Joseph* from *The Wild Knight and Other Poems* by Gilbert Keith Chesterton

Richard Church and William Heinemann Ltd., for *Christmas in the Indian Ocean* from *A Stroll Before Dark* by Richard Church

The Trustees of the Joseph Conrad Estate for *Christmas Day at Sea* from *Tales of Hearsay and Last Essays* by Joseph Conrad

David Daiches for *On the Twelfth Day of Christmas I Screamed*

Mrs. H. M. Davies for *Christmas* from *The Complete Poems of W. H. Davies* published by Jonathan Cape Ltd.

C. Day Lewis, the Hogarth Press Ltd., and Jonathan Cape Ltd., for *The Christmas Tree* from *Collected Poems 1954* by C. Day Lewis

Faber and Faber Ltd., for *Journey of the Magi* from *Collected Poems 1909–1962* by T. S. Eliot

Christy & Moore Ltd., for *Christmas at the South Pole* from *South With Scott* by E. R. G. R. Evans published by Wm. Collins Sons Ltd.

Natala de la Fère and Christy & Moore Ltd., for *The Mountains of Papa Morelli* from *Italian Bouquet* published by Thames and Hudson Ltd.

William Heinemann Ltd., for *Christmas and Conscience* from *Father and Son* by Edmond Gosse

Kenneth Grahame, The Bodleian Library Oxford and Methuen & Co., Ltd., for *Mole's Christmas* from *The Wind in the Willows* by Kenneth Grahame

Routledge & Kegan Paul Ltd., for *After Christmas* from *The Dual Site* by Michael Hamburger

Macmillan and Co., Ltd., and the Trustees of the Hardy Estate for *Going the Rounds* from *Under the Greenwood Tree; The 'Tivity Hymn* from *Tess of the D'Urbevilles;* and *The Oxen* from *The Collected Poems of Thomas Hardy*

Dorothy Hartley and Christy & Moore, Ltd., for *Boar's Head* from *Food In England* published by Macdonald & Co., Ltd.

Olwen Hedley and The Times for *Royal Christmasses at Windsor*

David Holbrook for *Delivering Children After a Party*

Winifred Holtby and Wm. Collins Sons Ltd., for *Mrs. Beddoes Receives a Christmas Present* from *South Riding* by Winifred Holtby

Rapp and Whiting Ltd., for *To Christ Our Lord* by Galway Kinnell

The Oxford University Press for *Prince for Your Coming* from *A Correct Compassion* by James Kirkup

Carla Lanyon Lanyon for *Carol*

Berta Lawrence and Westaway Books for *Wassailing in Somerset* from *A Somerset Journal* by Berta Lawrence

The Bodley Head and McClelland and Stewart Ltd., for *Hoodoo McFiggin's Christmas* from *Literary Lapses* by Stephen Leacock

Laurie Lee and John Lehmann Ltd., for *Christmas Landscape* from *The Bloom of Candles*

Rosamond Lehmann and The Society of Authors for *A Surprise Party* from *The Ballad and The Source* by Rosamond Lehmann

Sir Compton MacKenzie and Chatto & Windus Ltd., for *Five Years Old* from *My Life and Times: Octave One* by Compton MacKenzie

Edwin Morgan and The Times Literary Supplement for *The Computer's First Christmas Card*

Faber and Faber Ltd., for *Poem for Epiphany* from *Five Rivers* by Norman Nicholson

Eugene Kayden for the English translation of *Star of the Nativity* by Boris Pasternak

Mrs. Joyce Pearson for *Shaw and Christmas* from *Bernard Shaw: His Life and Personality* by Hesketh Pearson

S. J. Perelman for *Waiting for Santy* from *Crazy Like a Fox*

Frederick Warne and Co., Ltd., for *Simpkin's Christmas* from *The Tailor of Gloucester* by Beatrix Potter

The Estate of the Late John Cowper Powys for *Lubberlu*

A. D. Peters & Co., for *Miss Matfield and Christmas* from *Angel Pavement* by J. B. Priestley

Beatrice Scott for *Olya* from *On a Field Azure* by Remizov

William Kean Seymour for *Old Martha's Christmas, Yuletide, Christmas Scandal* and *Making the Most of It*

Randolph Stow and Macdonald & Co., Ltd., for *Australian Christmas* from *The Merry-Go-Round in the Sea*

John Smith for *Toward Bethelehem, The Next Day After Christmas* and *The Trouble with Presents*

The Trustees for the Copyrights of the Late Dylan Thomas for *Memories of Christmas* from *Quite Early One Morning* by Dylan Thomas

Gilbert Thomas for *Joseph* from *Selected Poems* published by Allen & Unwin Ltd.

Faber and Faber Ltd., for *Christmas is Coming* from *Country Things* by Alison Uttley

MacGibbon & Kee Ltd., for *The Gift* from *Pictures From Breughel* by William Carlos Williams

Geoffrey Willans and Max Parrish Ltd., for *Ding Dong Farely Merily for Xmas* from *How To Be Topp*

Rosalind Wade for *Christmas in Cornwall*

All the carols with music which appear in this anthology are reproduced by kind permission of the Oxford University Press

King George V's Christmas Broadcast is reproduced by gracious permission of Her Majesty The Queen

CONTENTS

BEFORE THE FEAST

CHRISTMAS EVE

CHRISTMAS DAY

AFTER THE FEAST

BEFORE THE FEAST

THE
COMPUTER'S
FIRST
CHRISTMAS
CARD

```
jollymerry
hollyberry
jollyberry
merryholly
happyjolly
jollyjelly
jellybelly
bellymerry
hollyheppy
jollyMolly
marryJerry
merryHarry
hoppyBarry
heppyJarry
boppyheppy
berryjorry
jorryjolly
moppyjelly
Mollymerry
Jerryjolly
bellyboppy
jorryhoppy
hollymoppy
Barrymerry
Jarryhappy
happyboppy
boppyjolly
jollymerry
merrymerry
merrymerry
merryChris
ammerryasa
Chrismerry
asMERRYCHR
YSANTHEMUM
```

Edwin Morgan

MUMMER RHYME

O Christmas is coming,
The geese are getting fat,
Won't you please put a penny
In a poor man's hat?
If you haven't got a penny
A ha'penny will do.
If you haven't got a ha'penny
Then God bless you!

Anon

CHERRY TREE CAROL

Joseph was an old man,
   And an old man was he,
When he wedded Mary
   In the land of Galilee.

Joseph and Mary walked
   Through an orchard good,
Where was cherries and berries
   So red as any blood.

Joseph and Mary walked
   Through an orchard green,
Where was berries and cherries
   As thick as might be seen.

O then bespoke Mary,
   So meek and so mild,
''Pluck me one cherry, Joseph,
   For I am with child.''

O then bespoke Joseph
   With words so unkind,
''Let him pluck thee a cherry
   That brought thee with child.''

O then bespoke the babe
    Within his mother's womb,
"Bow down then the tallest tree
    For my mother to have some."

Then bowed down the highest tree
    Unto his mother's hand:
Then she cried, "See, Joseph,
    I have cherries at command."

O then bespoke Joseph—
    "I have done Mary wrong;
But cheer up, my dearest,
    And be not cast down.

"O eat your cherries, Mary,
    O eat your cherries now;
O eat your cherries, Mary,
    That grow upon the bough."

Then Mary plucked a cherry
    As red as the blood;
Then Mary went home
    With her heavy load.

                                Anon

From "The Book of Days" edited by Robert Chambers

THE SEVEN JOYS OF MARY

THE "Advent Images" are two dolls, dressed the one to represent the Saviour and the other the Virgin Mary, and during the week before Christmas they are carried about the country by poor women who, in return for their exhibition, expect a halfpenny, which it is considered as ensuring the height of ill-luck to deny. The following carol is sung on the occasion by the bearers of the images:

The first good joy that Mary had, it was the joy of one,
To see her own son Jesus to suck at her breast-bone;
It brings tidings of comfort and joy.

The next good joy that Mary had, it was the joy of two,
To see her own son Jesus to make the lame to go.
It brings tidings of comfort and joy.

The next good joy that Mary had, it was the joy of three,
To see her own son Jesus to make the blind to see.
It brings tidings of comfort and joy.

The next good joy that Mary had, it was the joy of four,
To see her own son Jesus to read the Bible o'er.
It brings tidings of comfort and joy.

The next good joy that Mary had, it was the joy of five,
To see her own son Jesus to make the dead alive.
It brings tidings of comfort and joy.

The next good joy that Mary had, it was the joy of six,
To see her own son Jesus to bear the crucifix.
It brings tidings of comfort and joy.

The next good joy that Mary had, it was the joy of seven,
To see her own son Jesus to wear the crown of Heaven.
It brings tidings of comfort and joy.

This custom is also termed going about with a "vessel-cup", evidently a corruption for "wassail-cup".

From Kenneth Grahame's "The Wind in the Willows"

MOLE'S CHRISTMAS

THE Mole struck a match, and by its light the Rat saw that they were standing in an open space, neatly swept and sanded underfoot, and directly facing them was Mole's little front door, with "Mole End" painted, in Gothic lettering, over the bell-pull at the side.

Mole reached down a lantern from a nail on the wall and lit it, and the Rat, looking round him, saw that they were in a sort of forecourt. A garden-seat stood on one side of the door, and on the other, a roller; for the Mole, who was a tidy animal when at home, could not stand having his ground kicked up by other animals into little runs that ended in earth-heaps. On the walls hung wire baskets with ferns in them, alternating with brackets carrying plaster statuary—Garibaldi, and the infant Samuel, and Queen Victoria and other heroes of modern Italy. Down one side of the forecourt ran a skittle-alley, with benches along it and little wooden tables marked with rings that hinted of beer-mugs. In the middle was a small round pond containing goldfish and surrounded by a cockle-shell border.

Out of the centre of the pond rose a fanciful erection clothed in more cockle-shells and topped by a large silvered glass ball that reflected everything all wrong and had a very pleasing effect.

Mole's face beamed at the sight of all these objects so dear to him, and he hurried Rat through the door, lit a lamp in the hall, and took one glance round his old home. He saw the dust lying thick on everything, saw the cheerless, deserted look of the long-neglected house, and its narrow, meagre dimensions, its worn and shabby contents—and collapsed again on a hall-chair, his nose in his paws. "O, Ratty!" he cried dismally, "why ever did I do it? Why did I bring you to this poor, cold little place, on a night like this, when you might have been at River Bank by this time, toasting your toes before a blazing fire, with all your own nice things about you!"

The Rat paid no heed to his doleful self-reproaches. He was running here and there, opening doors, inspecting rooms and cupboards, and lighting lamps and candles and sticking them up everywhere. "What a capital little house this is!" he called out cheerily. "So compact! So well planned! Everything here and everything in its place! We'll make a jolly night of it. The first thing we want is a good fire; I'll see to that—I always know where to find things. So this is the parlour? Splendid! Your own idea, those little sleeping-bunks in the wall? Capital! Now, I'll fetch the wood and the coals, and you get a duster, Mole—you'll find one in the drawer of the kitchen table—and try and smarten things up a bit. Bustle about, old chap!"

Encouraged by his inspiriting companion, the Mole roused himself and dusted and polished with energy and heartiness, while the Rat, running to and fro with armfuls of fuel, soon had a cheerful blaze roaring up the chimney. He hailed the Mole to come and warm himself; but Mole promptly had another fit of the blues, dropping down on a couch in dark despair and burying his face in his duster.

"Rat," he moaned, "how about your supper, you poor, cold, hungry, weary animal? I've nothing to give you—nothing—not a crumb!"

"What a fellow you are for giving in!" said the Rat reproachfully. "Why, only just now I saw a sardine-opener on the kitchen dresser, quite distinctly; and everybody knows that means there are sardines about somewhere in the neighbour-hood. Rouse yourself! pull yourself together, and come with me and forage."

They went and foraged accordingly, hunting through every cupboard and turning out every drawer. The result was not so very depressing after all, though of course it might have been better; a tin of sardines—a box of captain's biscuits, nearly full—and a German sausage encased in silver paper.

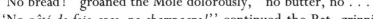

"There's a banquet for you!" observed the Rat, as he arranged the table. "I know some animals who would give their ears to be sitting down to supper with us to-night!"

"No bread!" groaned the Mole dolorously, "no butter, no . . ."

"No *pâté de foie gras, no champagne!*" continued the Rat, grinning. "And that reminds me – what's that little door at the end of the passage? Your cellar, of course! Every luxury in this house! Just you wait a minute.''

He made for the cellar door, and presently reappeared, somewhat dusty, with a bottle of beer in each paw and another under each arm. ''Self-indulgent beggar you seem to be, Mole,'' he observed. ''Deny yourself nothing. This is really the jolliest little place I ever was in. Now, wherever did you pick up those prints? Make the place look so home-like, they do. No wonder you're so fond of it, Mole. Tell us all about it, and how you came to make it what it is.''

Then, while the Rat busied himself fetching plates, and knives and forks, and mustard which he mixed in an egg-cup, the Mole, his bosom still heaving with the stress of his recent emotion, related—somewhat shyly at first, but with more freedom as he warmed to his subject—how this was planned, and how that was thought out, and how this was got through a windfall from an aunt, and that was a wonderful find and a bargain, and this other thing was bought out of laborious savings and a certain amount of ''going without''. His spirits finally quite restored, he must needs go and caress his possessions, and take a lamp and show off their points to his visitor and expatiate on them, quite forgetful of the supper they both so much needed; Rat, who was desperately hungry but strove to conceal it, nodding seriously, examining with a puckered brow, and saying, ''Wonderful,'' and ''Most remarkable,'' at intervals, when the chance for an observation was given him.

At last the Rat succeeded in decoying him to the table, and had just got seriously to work with the sardine-opener when sounds were heard from the fore-court without—sounds like the scuffling of small feet in the gravel and a confused murmur of tiny voices, while broken sentences reached them—''Now, all in a line—hold the lantern up a bit, Tommy—clear your throats first—no coughing after I say one, two, three.—Where's young Bill?—Here, come on, do, we're all a-waiting . . .''

''What's up?'' inquired the Rat, pausing in his labours.

''I think it must be the field-mice,'' replied the Mole, with a touch of pride in his manner. ''They go round carol-singing regularly at this time of the year. They're quite an institution in these parts. And they never pass me over—they come to 'Mole End' last of all; and I used to give them hot drinks, and supper too sometimes, when I could afford it. It will be like old times to hear them again.''

''Let's have a look at them!'' cried the Rat, jumping up and running to the door.

It was a pretty sight, and a seasonable one too, that met their eyes when they flung the door open. In the forecourt, lit by the dim rays of a horn-lantern, some eight or ten little field-mice stood in a semicircle, red worsted comforters round their throats, their forepaws thrust deep into their pockets, their feet jigging for warmth. With bright beady eyes they glanced shyly at each other, sniggering a little, sniffing and applying coat-sleeves a good deal. As the door opened, one of the older ones that carried the lantern was just saying, ''Now then, one, two, three!'' and forthwith their shrill little voices uprose on the air, singing one of the old-time carols that their forefathers composed in fields that were fallow and held by frost, or when snow-bound in chimney corners, and handed down to be snug in the miry street to lamp-lit windows at Yule-tide.

CAROL

Villagers all, this frosty tide,
Let your doors swing open wide,
Though wind may follow, and snow beside,
Yet draw us in by your fire to bide;
*   Joy shall be yours in the morning!*

Here we stand in the cold and the sleet,
Blowing fingers and stamping feet,
Come from far away you to greet—
You by the fire and we in the street—
*   Bidding you joy in the morning!*

For ere one half of the night was gone,
Sudden a star has led us on,
Raining bliss and benison—
Bliss to-morrow and more anon,
*   Joy for every morning!*

Goodman Joseph toiled through the snow—
Saw the star o'er a stable low;
Mary she might not further go—
Welcome thatch, and litter below!
*   Joy was hers in the morning!*

And then Mary heard the angels tell
'Who were the first to cry Nowell!
Animals all, as it befell,
In the stable where they did dwell!
*   Joy shall be theirs in the morning!'*

The voices ceased, the singers, bashful but smiling, exchanged sidelong glances, and silence succeeded—but for a moment only. Then, from up above and far away, down the tunnel they had so lately travelled was borne to their ears in a faint musical hum the sound of distant bells ringing a joyful and clangorous peal.

"Very well sung, boys!" cried the Rat heartily. "And now come along in, all of you, and warm yourselves by the fire, and have something hot!"

"Yes, come along, field-mice," cried the Mole eagerly. "This is quite like old times! Shut the door after you. Pull up that settle to the fire. Now, you just wait a minute, while we—O, Ratty!" he cried in despair, plumping down on a seat, with tears impending. "Whatever are we doing? We've nothing to give them!"

"You leave all that to me," said the masterful Rat. "Here, you with the lantern. Come over this way. I want to talk to you. Now, tell me, are there any shops open at this hour of the night?"

"Why, certainly, sir," replied the field-mouse respectfully. "At this time of the year our shops keep open to all sorts of hours."

"Then look here!" said the Rat. "You go off at once, you and your lantern, and you get me—"

Here much muttered conversation ensued, and the Mole only heard bits of it, such as—"Fresh, mind!—no, a pound of that will do—see you get Buggins's, for I won't have any other—no, only the best—if you can't get it there, try somewhere else—yes, of course, home-made, no tinned stuff—well then, do the best you can!" Finally, there was a chink of coin passing from paw to paw, the field-mouse was provided with an ample basket for his purchases, and off he hurried, he and his lantern.

The rest of the field-mice, perched in a row on the settle, their small legs swinging, gave themselves up to the enjoyment of the fire, and toasted their chilblains till they tingled; while the Mole, failing to draw them into easy conversation, plunged into family custom and made each of them recite the names of his numerous brothers, who were too young, it appeared, to be allowed to go out a-carolling this year, but looked forward very shortly to winning the parental consent.

The Rat, meanwhile, was busy examining the label on one of the beer-bottles. "I perceive this to be Old Burton," he remarked approvingly. "*Sensible* Mole! The very thing! Now we shall be able to mull some ale! Get the things ready, Mole, while I draw the corks."

It did not take long to prepare the brew and thrust the tin heater well into the red heart of the fire; and soon every field-mouse was sipping and coughing and choking (for a little mulled ale goes a long way) and wiping his eyes and laughing and forgetting he had ever been cold in all his life.

"They act plays too, these fellows," the Mole explained to the Rat. "Make them up all by themselves, and act them afterwards. And very well they do it, too! They gave us a capital one last year, about a field-mouse who was captured at sea by a Barbary corsair, and made to row in a galley; and when he escaped and got home again, his lady-love had gone into a convent. Here, you! You were in it, I remember. Get up and recite a bit."

The field-mouse addressed got up on his legs, giggled shyly, looked round the room, and remained absolutely tongue-tied. His comrades cheered him on, Mole coaxed and encouraged him, and the Rat went so far as to take him by the shoulders and shake him; but nothing could overcome his stage-fright. They were all busily engaged on him like watermen applying the Royal Humane Society's regulations to a case of long submersion, when the latch clicked, the door opened, and the field-mouse with the lantern reappeared, staggering under the weight of his basket.

There was no more talk of play-acting once the very real and solid contents of the basket had been tumbled out on the table. Under the generalship of Rat, everybody was set to do something or to fetch something. In a very few minutes supper was ready, and Mole, as he took the head of the table in a sort of dream, saw a lately barren board set thick with savoury comforts; saw his little friends' faces brighten and beam as they fell to without delay; and then let himself loose—for he was famished indeed—on the provender so magically provided, thinking what a happy home-coming this had turned out, after all. As they ate, they talked of old times, and the field-mice gave him the local gossip up to date, and answered as well as they could the hundred questions he had to ask them. The Rat said little or nothing, only taking care that each guest had what he wanted, and plenty of it, and that Mole had no trouble or anxiety about anything.

They clattered off at last, very grateful and showering wishes of the season, with their jacket pockets stuffed with remembrances for the small brothers and sisters at home. When the door had closed on the last of them and the chink of the lanterns had died away, Mole and Rat kicked the fire up, drew their chairs in, brewed themselves a last nightcap of mulled ale, and discussed the events of the long day. At last the Rat, with a tremendous yawn, said, "Mole, old chap, I'm ready to drop. Sleepy is simply not the word. That your bunk over on that side? Very well, then, I'll take this one. What a ripping little house this is! Everything so handy!"

He clambered into his bunk and rolled himself well up in the blankets, and slumber gathered him forthwith, as a swath of barley is folded into the arms of the reaping-machine.

The weary Mole also was glad to turn in without delay, and soon had his head on his pillow, in great joy and contentment.

OLD MARTHA'S CHRISTMAS

A week before the Christmas Feast
  Old Martha starts her annual game,
Cajoling one she calls the Least
  To join in worshipping the Name.
Last year she chose a mouse she'd seen
Careering round the soup tureen
  In which she keeps her crusts of bread.
  "He'll do me nicely," Martha said.

She trained him with a trail of crumbs
  Six nights to play her annual game,
Which carollers cried "Christmas Comes!
  O come and worship in Jesu's name!"—
So well that at her lonely feast
Old Martha shared it with the Least,
  But careful not to dance or sing
  For fear she'd frighten the wee thing.

This year I wonder whom she'll find
  To join her in her annual game?
A cockroach tempted by a rind,
  Or night-moth lured by candle flame?
Whoever comes she'll greet with joy
And murmur softly, "Darling boy,
  You've come to share my Christmas Feast
  And worship Jesus, you, the Least!"

William Kean Seymour

From J. B. Priestley's "Angel Pavement"

MISS MATFIELD AND CHRISTMAS

A DAY or two before Mr Golspie returned, Miss Matfield, sitting with cold feet and a novel she disliked in the 13 bus, realised with a shock that it was nearly Christmas. The shops she passed every day in the bus along Regent Street and Oxford Street had been celebrating Christmas for some time; and it was weeks since they had first broken out into their annual crimson rash of holly berries, robins, and Father Christmasses. The shops, followed by the illustrated papers, began it so early, with their full chorus of advertising managers and window-dressers, shouting, "Christmas is Here", at a time when it obviously wasn't, that when it did actually come creeping up, you had forgotten about it. Miss Matfield told herself this, and then remembered that every year her mother used to cry, "What, nearly Christmas already! I never thought it was so near. It's taken me completely by surprise this year." Yes, every year she used to say that, and year after year Miss Matfield would tease her about it. And now, Miss Matfield told herself, she had begun to say it, just as if she was on the point of becoming forgetful and absurd and middle-aged. Oh—foul! She stared out of the window. Those two miles of *Xmas Gifts* and lavish electric lighting and artificial holly leaves and cotton wool snow were still rolling past. The festive season—help! It was all an elaborate stunt to persuade everybody to spend money buying useless things for everybody else. . . .

It was, on the whole, she decided, revolting. You gave people a lot of silly things, diaries and calendars and rot, or useful things that were not right, gloves of the wrong size and stockings of the wrong shade (and she would have to be thinking out her presents now, and she was terribly hard up); and they in their turn gave you silly things and the useful things that were not right. You ate masses of food you didn't want (and even Dr Matfield, who had ideas about diet, said it didn't matter at Christmas), and then you sat about, pretending to be jolly, but really stodged, sleepy, headachy, and in urgent need of bicarbonate of soda. If you stayed at home, you yawned, tried to convince your mother that you hadn't a rich secret life you were hiding from her, and drearily sampled the family supply of literature. If you went out, you had to pretend you were having a marvellous time because you were wearing hats from crackers and playing pencil and paper games ("Let me see, a river beginning with a 'V'?"). And what was so terribly depressing and revolting about it all was that it was possible to imagine a really good Christmas, the adult equivalent of the enchanting Christmasses of childhood, the sort of Christmas that people always thought they were going to have and never did have. As the bus stopped by the dark desolation of Lord's cricket ground, swallowed two women who were all parcels, comic hats, and fuss (a sure sign this that Christmas was near, for you never saw these parcel-and-comic-hat women at any other time), and then rolled on, Miss Matfield took out from its secret recess that dream of a Christmas. She was in an old house in the country somewhere, with firelight and candlelight reflected in the polished wood surfaces; by her side, adoring her, was a vague figure, a husband, tall, strong, not handsome perhaps but distinguished, two or three children, vague too, nothing but laughter and a gleam of curls; friends arriving, delightful people—"Hello," they cried. "What a marvellous place you've got here! I *say*, Lilian!"; some smiling servants; logs on the fires, snow falling outside, old silver shining on the mahogany dining table, and "Darling, you look wonderful in that thing," said the masculine shadow in his deep thrilling voice. "Oh, you *fool*, stop it," Miss Matfield cried to herself. She had only brought out that nonsensical stuff to annoy herself. She liked reminding herself how silly she could be. It braced her.

Mr Golspie left for Paris—lucky man—on the morning of Christmas Eve; Mr Dersingham wished them all a merry Christmas and departed early; Mr Smeeth gave them all an extra week's money, brightened up a little, and hoped they would have a very good time. Miss Matfield, after working miracles, arrived at Paddington, a Paddington that suggested that some invading army had already reached the Bank and that shells were falling into Hyde Park and that the seat of government had already been transferred to Bristol, and she was just in time to get three-quarters of a seat and no leg space in the 5.46. The lights of Westbourne Park and Kensal Green, such as they were, blinked at her and then were gone. Thank God she was done with this nightmare of a London for a few days! Perhaps Christmas at home this time would be amusing. At any rate, it would be reasonable and quiet, and her father and mother would be glad to see her, and she would be glad to see them. As the train gathered speed, shrugging off the outer western suburbs, she thought of her parents with affection, and for a little time felt nearer the child she had once been, the child who had thought her father and mother so wonderful and had found Christmas the most radiant and magical season, than she had done for many a month. She closed her eyes, her mouth gradually lost its discontented curve; her whole face softened. Angel Pavement would hardly have recognized her.

JOURNEY OF THE MAGI

"A cold coming we had of it,
Just the worst time of the year
For a journey, and such a long journey:
The ways deep and the weather sharp,
The very dead of winter."
And the camels galled, sore-footed, refractory,
Lying down in the melting snow.
There were times we regretted
The summer palaces on slopes, the terraces,
And the silken girls bringing sherbet.
Then the camel men cursing and grumbling
And running away, and wanting their liquor and women,
And the night-fires going out, and the lack of shelters,
And the cities hostile and the towns unfriendly
And the villages dirty and charging high prices:
A hard time we had of it.

At the end we preferred to travel all night,
Sleeping in snatches,
With the voices singing in our ears, saying
That this was all folly.
Then at dawn we came down to a temperate valley,
Wet, below the snow line, smelling of vegetation;
With a running stream and a water-mill beating the darkness,
And three trees on the low sky,
And an old white horse galloped away in the meadow.
Then we came to a tavern with vine-leaves over the lintel,
Six hands at an open door dicing for pieces of silver,
And feet kicking the empty wine-skins.
But there was no information, and so we continued
And arrived at evening, not a moment too soon
Finding the place; it was (you may say) satisfactory.

All this was a long time ago, I remember,
And I would do it again, but set down
This set down
This: were we led all that way for
Birth or Death? There was a Birth, certainly,
We had evidence and no doubt. I had seen birth and death,
But had thought they were different; this Birth was
Hard and bitter agony for us, like Death, our death.
We returned to our places, these Kingdoms,
But no longer at ease here, in the old dispensation,
With an alien people clutching their gods.
I should be glad of another death.

T. S. Eliot

TOWARD BETHLEHEM

It is so far, Mary said: oh how many hundred miles
Have we laboured, arguing over and over, it is too far?
The child with its low wail is angry and eager for life;
Though if it knew what a death this life is it might turn back
Even now in a miraculous retraction and unbind us
From the stark terror, the dull ache of this journey.
If we had asked to be blessed thus I should say:
"We will find a birthplace though a sea burst out before us."
But, as it is, surely some village we passed would have sufficed?
We could have rested there. One more sin, Joseph, on your head,
Would not count much in the long run; you've sinned enough already.

So the long trek went on; always the storm
Hung over their heads. The petty bickering that broke out
At every turn in the road frayed the narrow rope
Of reason and good will. At last they separated
And tramped in merciful silence, sullenly apart,
With Mary weeping under the too fierce sun.

Toward evening of a day they came to the place. The story
Is well known how, beaten at last, they crawled into a stable
And slept among the straw; after all the pain there was nothing
To ease the agony or bring a little joy to their side.
Joseph, bitter at first, found comfort after the birth.
The miracle, flowering under his eyes, warmed his chill heart.
And Mary? Well perhaps the delirium, the hot fever,
That racked and twisted her face to an old woman's face,
Opened a little door hidden at the back of the mind
And let a little happiness creep in
With a sound of Angels singing, and a glimpse of God.

John Smith

MERRY CHRISTMAS

Christmas comes! He comes, he comes,
Ushered with a rain of plums;
Hollies in the window greet him;
Schools come driving post to meet him;
Gifts precede him, bells proclaim him,
Every mouth delights to name him;
Wet, and cold, and wind, and dark,
Make him but the warmer mark;
And yet he comes not one-embodied,
Universal's the blithe godhead,
And in every festal house
Presence hath ubiquitous.
Curtains, those snug room-enfolders,
Hang upon his million shoulders,
And he has a million eyes
Of fire, and eats a million pies,
And is very merry and wise;
Very wise and very merry,
And loves a kiss beneath the berry.

Leigh Hunt

From Rosamond Lehmann's "The Ballad and the Source"

A SURPRISE PARTY

ONE afternoon in Christmas week, 1916, a motor-bicycle roared up to the front door, and a young man in khaki dismounted. From the schoolroom window we saw him run up the steps in a debonair way and press the bell. Who could this be, we asked ourselves, half aghast, so intrepid, so ignorant as not to know that nobody came so lightly to our door any more? Shortly afterwards Mossop appeared in the schoolroom, and announced a gentleman to see us in the drawing-room. To see us! . . . We blushed, ran combs through our hair, and in a twitter descended. A tall, fair, pink young man with sentimental blue eyes, an untidy mouth, and an expression of simple goodwill, stood beaming at us. It was Malcolm, in the uniform of a subaltern in the Gunners. He was just eighteen. At seventeen he had decided to leave school and join the army. A month ago he had got his commission, he expected shortly to go abroad. He had a few days' Christmas leave, and Maisie had hit on the notion of their wiring for Harry's permission to spend it at the Priory. So there they were: one wing had been taken out of dust sheets, and they were having a glorious picnic, with Maisie and Mrs Gillman sharing the housework. There was a sort of party to-morrow night: some friends were turning up. Could we be persuaded to come to supper and stay the night?

The night came down in a noiseless eternity of wet, part fog, part rain: a nasty night for the road; and horrors! our mother underwent a dubious period. The suffocation of our anxiety did not relax until we had climbed up and round the sweep of the drive. Then we were standing in the porch, prey to a clutch even more complex and acute; and the headlights, shafts of some silvery, half-solid substance, tunnelling with difficulty through a world of luminous midge swarms, wheeled away. We stood in blanketing dark with our suitcases, and heard the bell peal, and felt the damp stick to our hands, our faces. Then we heard steps coming with a run and a buoyant leap, the door burst open, Malcolm was before us, radiant, solid, reassuring under the five-branched wrought-iron lamp of the outer hall. Once more we stepped in over the blue and white mosaic paving into the body of Mrs Jardine's house.

"Oh, grand!" He was voluble, hospitable, helping us off with our coats. "This filthy night—ghastly doubts were beginning to gnaw me. Do you want to go straight upstairs according to Maisie's instructions? No, you don't. You look as neat as a packet of new pins. Marvellous!"

We stood revealed in our long-sleeved velvets—Jess's sapphire blue, mine claret-coloured, cut by local Miss Midgley with more optimism, fitted and finished

with more complacency than the results warranted. We wore our pearl initial christening brooches, and our gold lockets, and our long hair was tied back with wide, stiff, moire ribbon to match.

"I'm butler-valet to-night," he said. "There's no knowing what might happen. My hat, isn't this fun? I've got a gramophone, so we can dance, Maisie's cooking, she said to bring you to the kitchen, I hope you don't mind. We've all been chucking different things into the saucepans—you never saw such a mess. We thought we'd better send Mrs Gillman home, she was beginning to look a trifle pinched about the mouth. She's presented us with an outsize in Christmas puddings she made last year and never used, so we can always fall back on that. It's fairly stuffed with pre-war richnesses." He led the way along the passage towards the back premises. His hair was a little dishevelled, his tunic unbuttoned, his face Leander pink. "I shot a brace of pheasants yesterday," he said. "D'you suppose they'll be tough? Maisie says she knows how to deal with 'em. Actually we've torn them in pieces and bunged them into a giant's stew-pot, and Gil poured a bottle of red wine over them, so I don't know," he said again, hilarious, "what mightn't happen. . . . Maisie! Here they are."

We stood in the kitchen doorway, assailed by what seemed to my giddy senses a roaring pantomime cavern of light and colour. Brilliance, decoration, steam, smells streamed towards us. The dresser was festooned with holly and evergreens, in the middle distance stood a vast table heaped with utensils, with bowls, bottles, loaves, apples, Brussels sprouts, and, surmounting all, a toppling, drifting pile of dark feathers. Over this extravagant composition a bunch of mistletoe tied on a string to a hook in the ceiling spread its chill, glistening, porcelain-bead-studded, abstract convolutions. Beyond loomed a figure stooping over the range: a short stocky female figure swathed in a long cook's apron with a bib and cross-straps.

"Oh, hallo, you've come!"

YULE-TIDE

Roman Saturnalia,
  Christian Adoration,
Ivy wreath of Thalia,
  Druid exaltation.

Spruce and fir and myrtle;
  Mithras, God of Light;
How the yule-logs spurtle,
  Blaze for Christmas Night!

Yule, or Jul (from Caesar:
  Others claim Demeter—
Hymn they sang to please her,
  Every graceful eater);

Giul or hiul (for *wheel*ing
  Winter orb of light):
Shadows wreathe the ceiling,
  Dance on Christmas Night.

Ritual Germanic,
  Gothic and Moravian,
Persian and Romanic,
  Greek and Scandinavian.

Oel (or *ale* in plenty),
  Yule log blazing bright:
Dolce far niente,
  Joy this Christmas Night.

Pagan Saturnalia,
  Christian Adoration.
Christ—and Sun—the Saviour,
  Hear our Salutation!

William Kean Seymour

From Hilaire Belloc's "Mrs Markham's New History of England"

MRS MARKHAM ON CHRISTMAS

MARY: *(settling down comfortably)* And now, dear Mamma, you will tell us something about Christmas, as you promised.

MAMMA: Well, my dear, I suppose I must, because the Season of Good Will and Peace on Earth is approaching; but I confess I prefer to instruct you children in the workings of our Constitution, the justice of our Laws and the beautiful adaptations of our Social System, which is the pride and envy of the world.

TOMMY: Yes, dear Mamma, and on the foreign policy of our beloved country and its dealings with inferior races. I vow and protest but for your instruction—

MARY: Do stop him, Mamma! We shall never get to Christmas if he goes on like this.

TOMMY: Stop yourself! I was only thanking Mamma for her intensely interesting information.

MARY: You weren't! You were using long words. You love the sound of your own voice.

MAMMA: Children! Children! This will never do! Here we are, nearer every day to the great feast and Boxing Day succeeding it, and it is shocking to mar its holy calm with wrangling and cursing.

TOMMY: But, Mamma! I didn't curse. I didn't even say—

MARY: Oh! Mamma, he's going to say that dreadful word again!

MAMMA: *(sharply)* Quiet! *(She smoothes her skirts)* I desire you, I command you both to sit silent while I describe to you the origin and character of Christmas . . . Christmas, my dears, is the mid-winter feast of us English folk and one to which we have always been lovingly attached. Our Saxon Forefathers knew it as Yule-tide and would hold Wassail in Hall with song and foaming cups of Mead.

TOMMY: *(very interested)* What is Mead, Mamma?

MAMMA: Mead, my dear, is a fermented liquor made with Honey.

TOMMY: Supposing I were to take some Honey and Hot Water, Mamma, and . . .

MARY:	*(interrupting him)* Was it intoxicating, Mamma?
MAMMA:	No doubt it was mildly exhilarating as befitted occasions of rejoicing, but not strictly speaking intoxicating.
MARY:	It would be horrible to think of them getting drunk!
TOMMY:	Who?
MAMMA:	She is speaking of our Saxon Forefathers, Tommy. We must remember that they were ruder than we are, for all get better as time goes on, but they were of the same sturdy stuff as we are and had the same self-control and decency, so I am sure they never got drunk—a horrible idea, as you rightly say.
MARY:	Why did they sit in the Hall, Mamma? Why did they not drink in the Dining Room?
MAMMA:	My dear, in those days the Hall *was* the Dining Room. Everyone took dinner in the Hall.
TOMMY:	What an extraordinary place to dine in!
MAMMA:	Yet so it was: and all classes—Lords and Ladies and guests and servants all dined together.
MARY:	*(starting)* Oh! Mamma! Incredible! Do you really mean that the maids, like our Anne and Evangeline, came upstairs and ate with Gentlemen and Ladies, and even Lords?
MAMMA:	Yes, my dear; it was indeed the case. But, as I have told you, they were still in a rude condition, so perhaps there was not so much difference between the Upper and Lower Classes as there is today.
MARY:	What does Lady mean, Mamma?
MAMMA:	Wise men tell us that it means "Loaf Giver".
MARY:	How do they know, Mamma?
MAMMA:	They do not tell us, my dear, and it would ill become us to enquire. We must humbly accept their information—and there is much else of the kind. For instance, "Book" comes from the habit of writing on Beech Bark, and "Horse" is derived from a word meaning "Mare", while "Beef" comes from "Ox". *(A long silence).* *(after a further pause)* Well! Well!
MARY:	Pray, Mamma, why do we hang holly and other evergreens about the House and even in Church at Christmas?
MAMMA:	As an accompaniment to our festivity, my dear, I suppose, or perhaps as a sign of our rejoicing. It is a most ancient custom.
MARY:	*(doubtfully)* I see; and the same with Christmas Trees.
MAMMA:	No. Those are of recent introduction and come, like most good things, from Germany. They were brought into England by Albert the Good.
TOMMY:	Pray, who was this foreign potentate, Mamma?

MAMMA: *(sighing)* Ah! My children! He is no longer a name to your generation! To mine he was a sacred memory, and dear Granny actually saw him with her own eyes.

TOMMY: *(persisting)* Yes! But who was he, Mamma?

MAMMA: He was a German Prince, the Husband of our Great Queen Victoria.

MARY: Great Heavens! I never knew Queen Victoria ever had a husband!

MAMMA: Of course she had, my dear, but he died, alas! comparatively early in life.

TOMMY: Why was he so good, Mamma?

MAMMA: Because he had a good mother. She was also a very clever woman, as German women so often are, and had many brilliant friends attending her; among others a Mr Meyer, from whom little Albert may have acquired his fine taste in pictures.

MARY: Was he handsome, Mamma?

MAMMA: Strikingly so, I believe. But I can only judge from his monuments, which hardly do him justice . . . Well, then, he it was who grafted the Christmas Tree on to our dear old English Christmas. He also introduced Fish Knives.

CHRISTMAS

The bells of waiting Advent ring,
    The Tortoise stove is lit again
And lamp-oil light across the night
    Has caught the streaks of winter rain
In many a stained-glass window sheen
From Crimson Lake to Hooker's Green.

The holly in the windy hedge
    And round the Manor House the yew
Will soon be stripped to deck the ledge,
    The altar, font and arch and pew,
So that the villagers can say
"The church looks nice" on Christmas Day.

Provincial public houses blaze,
    And Corporation tramcars clang,
On lighted tenements I gaze
    Where paper decorations hang,
And bunting in the red Town Hall
Says "Merry Christmas to you all."

And London shops on Christmas Eve
    Are strung with silver bells and flowers
As hurrying clerks the City leave
    To pigeon-haunted classic towers,
And marbled clouds go scudding by
The many-steepled London sky.

And girls in slacks remember Dad,
    And oafish louts remember Mum,
And sleepless children's hearts are glad,
    And Christmas-morning bells say "Come!"
Even to shining ones who dwell
Safe in the Dorchester Hotel.

And is it true? And is it true,
    This most tremendous tale of all,
Seen in a stained-glass window's hue,
    A Baby in an ox's stall?
The Maker of the stars and sea
Become a Child on earth for me?

And is it true? For if it is,
    No loving fingers tying strings
Around those tissued fripperies,
    The sweet and silly Christmas things,
Bath salts and inexpensive scent,
And hideous tie so kindly meant,

No love that in a family dwells,
    No carolling in frosty air,
Nor all the steeple-shaking bells
    Can with this single Truth compare—
That God was Man in Palestine
And lives to-day in Bread and Wine.

John Betjeman

From Randolph Stow's "The Merry-go-round in the Sea"
AUSTRALIAN CHRISTMAS 1941

IT began to be nearly Christmas, and the boy's Aunt Judith came to stay with Grandma, bringing two girl-cousins too small to be interesting. Aunty Judith had a soothing laugh which made him feel comfortable. Now Grandma was cooking things all the time, making cakes and biscuits, and when she had finished with the basins she put them on a table out on the lawn, so that Rob and Nan and the cousins could "lick the basin", running their fingers round the basins and licking them. They were a trial to Grandma, who was hot in front of the wood-stove, but she let them make dough-men and bake them in the oven. And when she got tired of the children she would give them each a biscuit with a face on it, made of currants, and say: "Now, run away laughing." They called the biscuits run-away laughings. "Grandma, can I have a run-away-laughing?"

In the mornings Aunt Kay made toast in front of the wood-stove holding a newspaper before her face to keep off the heat. Aunt Kay's face got red in the light from the jamwood logs. The wood smelled like raspberry jam when it lay on the hearth, and like toast when it was burning.

On Christmas Eve the boy could not sleep. The pillowslip hung at the bed-end gaping for presents, and he lay listening to the sea. Then he heard his father and mother coming, creeping, or trying to creep, but his father's big boots made a noise like chopping wood. He heard the rustle of presents going into the pillowslip, and lay with his eyes closed, giggling inside, thinking: "Father Christmas wears Army boots." He had half a mind to tell them that he knew about Father Christmas.

The morning was rustling parcels, the smell of new presents, the soap-smell that Grandma Coram's presents always had, bright string and paper. They went to dinner at Grandma's, the big table in the dining room surrounded by relations. The cousins compared presents, coveted presents, offered to swap presents, and fought. The cousins belonging to Susan had presents from Rick, and the boy was jealous. He only had a present which said: "From Aunt Mary and Uncle Ernest and Rick."

In the evening the grown-ups sat in deck-chairs in the cool, and the children crawled and rolled on the fresh lawn. Rob sat in the grass beside Aunt Kay and played with a toy merry-go-round which made music as it turned. It belonged to his cousin Jenny, and he did not intend to give it back.

The grown-ups were talking, a quiet sound in the background of the tinkling music. One word they kept saying again and again. He repeated it to himself. "Hong Kong," he said, listening to it. "Hong Kong." He giggled inside. It was such a goofy sound.

One night the boy woke in the dark, and the world had gone mad and screaming.

There were roaring, screaming sounds in the night, then shriller, sharper, multi-tudinous screaming sounds closer at hand. From the drawing-room came loud voices.

He got up in the dark and ran, running towards the lighted drawing-room, which was full of ladies and men and soldiers, standing up and drinking from glasses and kissing each other.

He stood in the doorway in his pyjamas, and his mother came towards him, with blue eyes.

"What's the matter, Rob?" she said, bending down to him. "Did you have a nasty old nightgown?"[1]

"No," he said, breathing shakily. "It's the noises."

"Oh, that's just grown-ups being silly," his mother said. "The ships are blowing their sirens and people are tooting their car-horns because it's New Year."

"What's New Year?" said the boy, still trembling.

"Well, it's a different year from last year, with a different number. Yesterday it was 1941, and today it's 1942."

"Happy New Year, Robbie," someone called.

He stood in his pyjamas thinking about it, until it seemed to make sense. Happy New Year. 1942 was a happy new year, and people were tooting their horns, getting ready to be happy. 1941 was a sad year, when Rick had gone away. Now they were going to be happy, and Rick would have to come back again, because there was only one place to be happy, and that was here.

[1]nightmare

CHRISTMAS IS A BUSY TIME

Get ivy and hull,[1] woman, deck up thine house,
And take this same brawn for to seethe and to souse;
Provide us good cheer, for thou knowest the old guise,
Old customs that good be, let no man despise.
At Christmas be merry and thank God of all,
And feast thy poor neighbours, the great and the small.
Yea, all the year long have an eye to the poor,
And God shall send luck to keep open thy door.
Good fruit and good plenty do well in thy loft,
Then lay for an orchard and cherish it oft.
The profit is mickle, the pleasure is much;
At pleasure with profit few wise men will grutch.[2]
For plants and for stocks lay aforehand to cast,
But set or remove them, while Twelve-tide do last.

Thomas Tusser

[1] holly   [2] grouch

From Dorothy Wordworth's Journal

CHRISTMAS AT GRASMERE

DECEMBER 20th, *Sunday*. [1801] – It snowed all day. It was a very deep snow. The brooms were very beautiful, arched feathers with wiry stalks pointed to the end, smaller and smaller. They waved gently with the weight of the snow.

21st, *Monday*. Being the shortest day. Mary walked to Ambleside for letters. It was a wearisome walk, for the snow lay deep upon the roads and it was beginning to thaw. I stayed at home. Wm. sat beside me, and read *The Pedlar*. He was in good spirits, and full of hope of what he should do with it. He went to meet Mary, and they brought four letters—two from Coleridge, one from Sara, and one from France. Coleridge's were melancholy letters. He had been very ill. We were made very unhappy. Wm. wrote to him, and directed the letter into Somersetshire. I finished it after tea. In the afternoon Mary and I ironed.

22nd, *Tuesday*. Wm. composed a few lines of *The Pedlar*. We talked about Lamb's tragedy[1] as we went down the White Moss. We stopped a long time in going to watch a little bird with a salmon-coloured breast, a white cross or T upon its wings, and a brownish back with faint stripes. It began to peck upon the road at

[1] His sister Mary's insanity

the distance of four yards from us, and advanced nearer and nearer till it came within the length of W's stick, without any apparent fear of us. I found Mary at home in her riding-habit, all her clothes being put up. We were very sad about Coleridge. We sate snugly round the fire. I read to them the Tale of Custance and the Syrian Monarch, in the *Man of Lawe's Tale*, also some of the *Prologues*.

23rd, *Wednesday*. Mary wrote out the Tales from Chaucer for Coleridge. William worked at *The Ruined Cottage* and made himself very ill. A broken soldier came to beg in the morning.

24th, *Thursday*. Still a thaw. Wm., Mary, and I sate comfortably round the fire in the evening and read Chaucer. Thoughts of last year. I took out my old Journal.

25th, *Friday*. Christmas Day. We received a letter from Coleridge. His letter made us uneasy about him. I was glad I was not by myself when I received it.

26th, *Saturday*. We walked to Rydale. Grasmere Lake a beautiful image of stillness, clear as glass, reflecting all things, the wind was up, and the waters sounding. The lake of a rich purple, the fields a soft yellow, the island yellowish-green, the copses red brown, the mountains purple. The Church and buildings, how quiet they were! Poor Coleridge, Sara, and dear little Derwent were here last year at this time. After tea we sate by the fire comfortably. I read aloud *The Miller's Tale*. Wrote to Coleridge. William wrote part of the poem to Coleridge.[1]

27th, *Sunday*. A fine soft beautiful, mild day, with gleams of sunshine. William went to take in his boat. I sate in John's Grove a little while. Mary came home. Mary wrote some lines of the third part of Wm.'s poem, which he brought to read to us, when we came home.

28th, *Monday*. William, Mary, and I set off on foot to Keswick. We carried some cold mutton in our pockets, and dined at John Stanley's, where they were making Christmas pies. The sun shone, but it was coldish. We parted from Wm. upon the Rays. He joined us opposite Sara's rock. He was busy in composition, and sate down upon the wall. We did not see him again till we arrived at John Stanley's. There we roasted apples in the oven. After we had left John Stanley's, Wm. discovered that he had lost his gloves. He turned back, but they were gone. We rested often. Once he left his Spenser, and Mary turned back for it, and found it upon the bank, where we had last rested. We reached Greta Hall at about half past 5 o'clock.

29th, *Tuesday*. A fine morning. A thin fog upon the hills which soon disappeared. The sun shone. Wilkinson went with us to the top of the hill. We turned out of the road at the second mile stone, and passed a pretty cluster of houses at the foot of St. John's Vale. The houses were among tall trees, partly of Scotch fir, and some naked forest trees. We crossed a bridge just below these houses, and the river winded sweetly along the meadows. Our road soon led us along the sides of dreary bare hills, but we had a glorious prospect to the left of Saddleback, half-way covered with snow, and underneath the comfortable white houses and

[1] a first version of '*The Ruined Cottage*'

the village of Threlkeld. These houses and the village want trees about them. Skiddaw was behind us, and dear Coleridge's desert home. As we ascended the hills it grew very cold and slippery. Luckily, the wind was at our backs, and helped us on. A sharp hail-shower gathered at the head of Martindale, and the view upwards was very grand—the wild cottages, seen through the hurrying hail-shower. The wind drove, and eddied about and about, and the hills looked large and swelling through the storm. We thought of Coleridge. O! the bonny

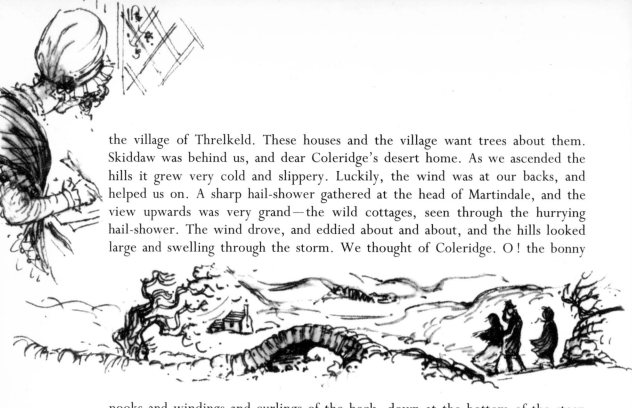

nooks and windings and curlings of the beck, down at the bottom of the steep green mossy banks. We dined at the public-house on porridge, with a second course of Christmas pies.

The landlord went about a mile and a half with us to put us in the right way. The road was often very slippery, the wind high, and it was nearly dark before we got into the right road. I was often obliged to crawl on all fours, and Mary fell many a time. A stout young man whom we met on the hills, and who knew Mr Clarkson, very kindly set us into the right road, and we inquired again near some houses, and were directed by a miserable, poverty-struck looking woman, who had been fetching water, to go down a nasty miry lane. We soon got into the main road and reached Mr Clarkson's at tea-time.

December 24th, Christmas Eve [1802]. William is now sitting by me, at half-past ten o'clock. I have been repeating some of his sonnets to him, listening to his own repeating, reading some of Milton's, and the *Allegro* and *Penseroso*. It is a quiet keen frost. Coleridge came this morning with Wedgwood. We all turned out one by one, to meet him. He looked well. We had to tell him of the birth of his little girl, born yesterday morning at six o'clock. Wm. went with them to Wytheburn in the chaise, and M. and I met W. on the Rays. It was not an unpleasant morning. The sun shone now and then, and there was no wind, but all things looked chearless and distinct; no meltings of sky into mountains, the mountains like stone work wrought up with huge hammers.

It is to-day Christmas Day, Saturday, 25th December 1802. I am thirty-one years of age. It is a dull, frosty day.

MRS BEDDOWS RECEIVES A CHRISTMAS PRESENT

L IFE at Willow Lodge moved through a cycle of festivities—Christmas, Easter, Whitsun and the Summer Holidays—with smaller feast-days interspersed between them, horse-shows, bazaars, the Flintonbridge Point-to-Point, the High School Speech Days.

But of all these focal points the most active, persistent and inescapable was Christmas. The season began almost as soon as the little boys ran round the Kiplington streets shouting "Penny for the Old Guy" on frosty November evenings; long before notices went up in the lighted Kingsport windows, "PLEASE SHOP EARLY", its imminence overshadowed all other Beddows' activities; it rose slowly to its climax with the carving of the family turkey at midday dinner on Christmas Day, and subsided gradually through Boxing Day, the maids' holidays, indigestion and crumbling evergreen decorations until the old calendars could be thrown away, the garlands taken down, and the New Year had come.

The normal ardours and endurances of a Christmas season were multiplied twenty-fold for Mrs Beddows by her own temperament and her husband's parsimony. It was true that since Willie came to live with her she had had a little money to spend upon her benefactions. But her heart was so generous, her range of acquaintance so wide and delight in human relationships so unstaled, that she could have spent a national income without difficulty. As it was, she was put to desperate straits to accommodate her lavish tastes to her narrow fortune.

All through the year she and her family set themselves to accumulate the objects which she could bestow as gifts at Christmas. In a chest on the front landing known as the "glory hole" they stored the harvest of bazaars and birthdays, of raffles, bridge-drive parties, bargain sales, and even presents which they had themselves received at former Christmases. Into the glory hole went blotters, pen-wipers, and painted vases, dessert d'oylies, table-centres and imitation fruits of wax or velvet, lamp-shades, knitted bed-jackets and embroidered covers for the *Radio Times*, all the bric-a-brac of civil exchange or time-killing occupation. The indictment of a social system lay in those drawers if they but knew it—a system which overworks eight-tenths of its female population, and gives the remaining two-tenths so little to do that they must clutter the world with useless objects. Mrs Beddows did not see it quite like that; presents were presents; bazaars were bazaars, and Sybil was teaching the Women's Institute class raffia work and glove-making. Surely these were good things? She did not question further.

Early in the month the contents of the glory hole were brought down into the dining-room and sorted. Aunt Ursula's plant pot might do for the Rectory people;

but Mr Peckover's framed verse ("A garden is a lovesome thing, God wot") must not be sent to Dr Dale. All last year's donors must be this year's recipients, but once the known debts were honourably fulfilled, the real excitement of the season started. As cards, hair-tidies and markers began to arrive by every post, they were checked against the list of out-going presents, and consternation reigned in Willow Lodge if it were found that Cousin Rose, who had sent a cut-glass vase, had been rewarded only by three coat-hangers in a cretonne case. Unexpected gifts sent the family ransacking drawers and cupboards to find suitable QPQ's (Beddows' jargon for "quid pro quos"). The nearer the approach to Christmas Day itself, the lower ran the supply of possible exchanges, until finally even this year's presents were hastily repacked and despatched again hot from the post, with cards altered and brown paper readdressed.

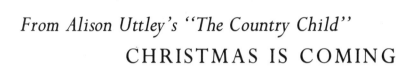

From Alison Uttley's "The Country Child"

CHRISTMAS IS COMING

AT Christmas the wind ceased to moan. Snow lay thick on the fields and the woods cast blue shadows across it. The fir trees were like sparkling, gem-laden Christmas trees, the only ones Susan had ever seen. The orchard, with the lacy old boughs outlined with snow, was a grove of fairy trees. The woods were enchanted, exquisite, the trees were holy, and anything harmful had shrunken to a thin wisp and had retreated into the depths.

The fields lay with their unevennesses gone and paths obliterated, smooth white slopes criss-crossed by black lines running up to the woods. More than ever the farm seemed under a spell, like a toy in the forest, with little wooden animals and men; a brown horse led by a stiff little red-scarfed man to a yellow stable door; round, white, woolly sheep clustering round a blue trough of orange mangolds; red cows drinking from a square white trough, and returning to a painted cow-house.

Footprints were everywhere on the snow, rabbits and foxes, blackbirds, pheasants and partridges, trails of small paws, the mark of a brush, and the long feet of the cock pheasant and the tip-mark of his tail.

A jay flew out of the wood like a blue flashing diamond and came to the grass-plot for bread. A robin entered the house and hopped under the table while Susan sat very still and her father sprinkled crumbs on the floor.

Rats crouched outside the window, peeping out of the walls with gleaming eyes, seizing the birds' crumbs and scraps, and slowly lolloping back again.

Red squirrels ran along the walls to the back door, close to the window, to eat the crumbs on the bench where the milk-cans froze. Every wild animal felt that a truce had come with the snow, and they visited the house where there was food in plenty, and sat with paws uplifted and noses twitching.

For the granaries were full, it had been a prosperous year, and there was food for everyone. Not like the year before when there was so little hay that Mr Garland had to buy a stack in February. Three large haystacks as big as houses stood in the stackyard, thatched evenly and straight by Job Fletcher, who was the best thatcher for many a mile. Great mounds showed where the roots were buried. The brick-lined pit was filled with grains and in the barns were stores of corn.

The old brew-house was full of logs of wood, piled high against the walls, cut from trees which the wind had blown down. The coal-house with its strong ivied walls, part of the old fortress, had been stored with coal brought many a mile in the blaze of summer; twenty tons lay under the snow.

On the kitchen walls hung the sides of bacon and from hooks in the ceiling dangled great hams and shoulders. Bunches of onions were twisted in the pantry and barn, and an empty cow-house was stored with potatoes for immediate use.

The floor of the apple chamber was covered with apples, rosy apples, little yellow ones, like cowslip balls, wizenedy apples with withered, wrinkled cheeks, fat, well-fed, smooth-faced apples, and immense green cookers, pointed like a house, which would burst in the oven and pour out a thick cream of the very essence of apples.

Even the cheese chamber had its cheeses this year, for there had been too much milk for the milkman, and the cheese presses had been put into use again. Some of them were Christmas cheese, with layers of sage running through the middles like green ribbons.

Stone jars like those in which the forty thieves hid stood on the pantry floor, filled with white lard, and balls of fat tied up in bladders hung from the hooks. Along the broad shelves round the walls were pots of jam, blackberry and apple, from the woods and orchard, Victoria plum from the trees on house and barn, black currant from the garden, and red currant jelly, damson cheese from the half-wild ancient trees which grew everywhere, leaning over walls, dropping their blue fruit on paths and walls, in pig-sty and orchard, in field and water-trough, so that Susan thought they were wild as hips and haws.

Pickles and spices filled old brown pots decorated with crosses and flowers, like the pitchers and crocks of Will Shakespeare's time.

In the little dark wine chamber under the stairs were bottles of elderberry wine, purple, thick, and sweet, and golden cowslip wine, and hot ginger, some of them many years old, waiting for the winter festivities.

There were dishes piled with mince pies on the shelves of the larder, and a row of plum puddings with their white calico caps, and strings of sausages, and round pats of butter, with swans and cows and wheat-ears printed upon them.

Everyone who called at the farm had to eat and drink at Christmas-tide.

A few days before Christmas Mr Garland and Dan took a bill-hook and knife and went into the woods to cut branches of scarlet-berried holly. They tied them together with ropes and dragged them down over the fields to the barn. Mr Garland cut a bough of mistletoe from the ancient hollow hawthorn which leaned over the wall by the orchard, and thick clumps of dark-berried ivy from the walls.

Indoors, Mrs Garland and Susan and Becky polished and rubbed and cleaned the furniture and brasses, so that everything glowed and glittered. They decorated every room, from the kitchen where every lustre jug had its sprig in its mouth, every brass candlestick had its chaplet, every copper saucepan and preserving-pan had its wreath of shining berries and leaves, through the hall, which was a bower of

green, to the two parlours which were festooned and hung with holly and boughs of fir, and ivy berries dipped in red raddle, left over from sheep marking.

Holly decked every picture and ornament. Sprays hung over the bacon and twisted round the hams and herb bunches. The clock carried a crown on his head, and every dish-cover had a little sprig. Susan kept an eye on the lonely forgotten humble things, the jelly moulds and colanders and nutmeg-graters, and made them happy with glossy leaves. Everything seemed to speak, to ask for its morsel of greenery, and she tried to leave out nothing.

On Christmas Eve fires blazed in the kitchen and parlour and even in the bedrooms. Becky ran from room to room with the red-hot salamander which she stuck between the bars to make a blaze, and Mrs Garland took the copper warming-pan filled with glowing cinders from the kitchen fire and rubbed it between the sheets of all the beds. Susan had come down to her cosy tiny room with thick curtains at the window, and a fire in the big fireplace. Flames roared up the chimneys as Dan carried in the logs and Becky piled them on the blaze. The wind came back and tried to get in, howling at the keyholes, but all the shutters were cottered and the doors shut. The horses and mares stood in the stables, warm and happy, with nodding heads. The cows slept in the cow-houses, the sheep in the open sheds. Only Rover stood at the door of his kennel, staring up at the sky, howling to the dog in the moon, and then he, too, turned and lay down in his straw.

In the middle of the kitchen ceiling there hung the kissing-bunch, the best and brightest pieces of holly made in the shape of a large ball which dangled from the hook. Silver and gilt drops, crimson bells, blue glass trumpets, bright oranges and red polished apples, peeped and glittered through the glossy leaves. Little flags of all nations, but chiefly Turkish for some unknown reason, stuck out like quills on a hedgehog. The lamp hung near, and every little berry, every leaf, every pretty ball and apple had a tiny yellow flame reflected in its heart.

Twisted candles hung down, yellow, red, and blue, unlighted but gay, and on either side was a string of paper lanterns.

Mrs Garland climbed on a stool and nailed on the wall the Christmas texts, "God bless our Home", "God is Love", "Peace be on this House", "A Happy Christmas and a Bright New Year".

So the preparations were made. Susan hung up her stocking at the foot of the bed and fell asleep. But soon singing roused her and she sat, bewildered. Yes, it was the carol-singers.

Outside under the stars she could see the group of men and women, with lanterns throwing beams across the paths and on to the stable door. One man stood apart beating time, another played a fiddle and another had a flute. The rest sang in four parts the Christmas hymns, "While shepherds watched", "O come, all ye faithful", and "Hark the herald angels sing".

There was the Star, Susan could see it twinkling and bright in the dark boughs with their white frosted layers; and there was the stable. In a few hours it would be Christmas Day, the best day of all the year.

A NATIVITY SONG

How far is it to Bethlehem?
   Not very far.
Shall we find the stable-room
   Lit by a star?

Can we see the little child,
   Is he within?
If we lift the wooden latch
   May we go in?

May we stroke the creatures there,
   Ox, ass, or sheep?
May we peep like them and see
   Jesus asleep?

If we touch his tiny hand
   Will he awake?
Will he know we've come so far
   Just for his sake?

Great kings have precious gifts
   And we have naught,
Little smiles and little tears
   Are all we brought.

For all weary children
   Mary must weep.
Here, on his bed of straw
   Sleep, children, sleep.

God in his mother's arms,
   Babes in the byre,
Sleep, as they sleep who find
   Their heart's desire.

Frances Chesterton

A CHILD THIS DAY

Traditional

Arr. Geoffrey Shaw

The harmonies to verse 1 may be used throughout, if desired

With vigour

1. A child this day is born, A child of high re-nown, Most
2. These tid-ings shep-herds heard, In field watching their fold, Were

wor-thy of a scep-tre, A scep-tre and a crown:
by an an-gel un-to them That night re-veal'd and told:

CHORUS

Now-ell, Now-ell, Now-ell, Now-ell, sing all we may, Be-

Fine

-cause the King of all kings Was born this bless-ed day.
Be-cause the King Was born this day.

-cause the King of all kings Was born this bless-ed day.

3. To whom the an-gel spoke, Say-ing, 'Be not a-fraid; Be
4. 'For lo! I bring you tid-ings Of glad-ness and of mirth, Which

(Altos and Tenors, lightly)

Now-ell, Now-ell, Sing all we

56

glad, poor sil - ly shep - herds—Why are you so dis - mayed?'
com - eth to - all peo - ple by This ho - ly in - fant's birth':

may This bless - ed, This bless - ed, bless - ed day.

5. Then was there with the— an - gel An host in - con - ti - nent Of
7. And as the an - gel— told them, So to them did— ap - pear; They

dim.

hea - ven - ly bright sol - diers, Which from the High-est was sent:
found the young child, Je - sus Christ, With Ma - ry, his mo - ther dear:

6. Laud - ing the Lord our— God, And his ce - les - tial King; All

(Two bass parts) Now - ell,

Now - ell, Sing all_____ we

ff Now-

Now - ell,

Now-ell, Now - ell, } Now - -

glo - ry be in pa - ra - dise, This heav'n-ly host did sing:

may This bless - ed, This heav'n-ly host did sing. Now-

57

GOD REST YOU MERRY

Traditional, London

Traditional

1. God rest you mer-ry gen-tle-men, Let no-thing you dis-may, Re-
2. From God that is our Fa-ther, The bless-ed an-gels came, Un-

-mem-ber Christ our Sa-viour Was born on Christ-mas Day, To
-to some cer-tain shep-herds, With ti-dings of the same; That

save poor souls from Sa-tan's power Which had long time gone a-stray,)
there was born in Beth-le-hem, The___ Son of God by name.)

And it's

tid - ings of com - fort and joy, com-fort and joy: And it's

*joy.*___

tid - ings of com - fort and joy, com-fort and joy.

*joy.*___

58

3 Go, fear not, said God's angels,
   Let nothing you affright,
For there is born in Bethlehem,
   Of a pure virgin bright,
One able to advance you,
   And throw down Satan quite.
And it's tidings of comfort and joy.

4 The shepherds at those tidings,
   Rejoiced much in mind,
And left their flocks a feeding
   In tempest storms of wind,
And strait they came to Bethlehem,
   The Son of God to find.
And it's tidings of comfort and joy.

5 Now when they came to Bethlehem,
   Where our sweet Saviour lay,
They found him in a manger,
   Where oxen feed on hay,
The blessed Virgin kneeling down,
   Unto the Lord did pray.
And it's tidings of comfort and joy.

6 With sudden joy and gladness,
   The shepherds were beguil'd,
To see the Babe of Israel,
   Before his mother mild,
On them with joy and chearfulness,
   Rejoice each mother's child.
And it's tidings of comfort and joy.

7 Now to the Lord sing praises,
   All you within this place,
Like we true loving brethren,
   Each other to embrace,
For the merry time of Christmas,
   Is drawing on a pace.
And it's tidings of comfort and joy.

8 God bless the ruler of this house,
   And send him long to reign,
And many a merry Christmas
   May live to see again.
Among your friends and kindred,
   That live both far and near,
And God send you a happy New Year.

I SAW THREE SHIPS

Traditional

Traditional
Arr. Martin Shaw

4 Pray, whither sailed those ships all three?

5 O, they sailed into Bethlehem.

6 And all the bells on earth shall ring,

7 And all the angels in heaven shall sing,

8 And all the souls on earth shall sing.

9 Then let us all rejoice amain!

THE FIRST NOWELL

Traditional

Traditional
Arr. Martin Shaw

1. The first Nowell the angel did say Was to certain poor shepherds in fields as they lay; In fields where they lay, keeping their sheep, In a cold winter's night that was so deep: Nowell, Nowell, Nowell, Nowell, Born is the King of Israel!

2. They looked up and saw a star, Shining in the east, beyond them far; And to the earth it gave great light, And so it continued both day and night:

3 And by the light of that same star,
  Three wise men came from country far;
  To seek for a king was their intent,
  And to follow the star wheresoever it went:

  Nowell, etc.

4 This star drew nigh to the north-west;
  O'er Bethlehem it took its rest,
  And there it did both stop and stay
  Right over the place where Jesus lay:

  Nowell, etc.

5 *Then did they know assuredly
  Within that house the King did lie:
  One entered in then for to see,
  And found the babe in poverty:

  Nowell, etc.

6 Then entered in those wise men three,
  Fell reverently upon their knee,
  And offered there in his presénce
  Both gold and myrrh and frankincense:

  Nowell, etc.

7 *Between an ox-stall and an ass
  This child truly there born he was;
  For want of clothing they did him lay
  All in the manger, among the hay:

  Nowell, etc.

8 Then let us all with one accord
  Sing praises to our heavenly Lord,
  That hath made heaven and earth of naught,
  And with his blood mankind hath bought:

  Nowell, etc.

9 *If we in our time shall do well,
  We shall be free from death and hell;
  For God hath preparèd for us all
  A resting place in general:

  Nowell, etc.

CHRISTMAS
EVE

THE OXEN

Christmas Eve, and twelve of the clock.
    "Now they are all on their knees,"
An elder said as we sat in a flock
    By the embers in hearthside ease.

We pictured the meek mild creatures where
    They dwelt in their strawy pen,
Nor did it occur to one of us there
    To doubt they were kneeling then.

So fair a fancy few would weave
    In these years! Yet, I feel,
If someone said on Christmas Eve,
    "Come; see the oxen kneel

"In the lonely barton by yonder coomb
    Our childhood used to know,"
I should go with him in the gloom,
    Hoping it might be so. *Thomas Hardy*

From Thomas Hardy's "Under the Greenwood Tree"

GOING THE ROUNDS

SHORTLY after ten o'clock, the singing-boys arrived at the tranter's[1] house, which was invariably the place of meeting, and preparations were made for the start. The older men and musicians wore thick coats, with stiff perpendicular collars, and coloured handkerchiefs wound round and round the neck till the end came to hand, over all which they just showed their ears and noses, like people looking over a wall. The remainder, stalwart ruddy men and boys, were mainly dressed in snow-white smock-frocks, embroidered upon the shoulders and breasts, in ornamental form of hearts, diamonds, and zigzags. The cider-mug was emptied for the ninth time, the music-books were arranged and the pieces finally decided upon. The boys in the meantime put the old horn-lanterns in order, cut candles into short lengths to fit the lanterns; and a thin fleece of snow having fallen since the early part of the evening, those who had no leggings went to the stable and wound wisps of hay round their ankles to keep the insidious flakes from the interior of their boots.

Mellstock was a parish of considerable acreage, the hamlets composing it lying at a much greater distance from each other than is ordinarily the case. Hence several hours were consumed in playing and singing within hearing of every family, even if but a single air were bestowed on each. There was East Mellstock, the main village; half a mile from this were the church and the vicarage, called West Mellstock, and originally the most thickly-populated portion. A mile north-east lay the hamlet of Lewgate, where the tranter lived; and at other points knots of cottages, besides solitary farmsteads and dairies.

Old William Dewy, with the violoncello, played the bass; his grandson Dick the treble violin; and Reuben and Michael Mail the tenor and second violins respectively. The singers consisted of four men and seven boys, upon whom devolved the task of carrying and attending to the lanterns, and holding the books open for the players. Directly music was the theme, old William ever and instinctively came to the front.

"Now mind, naibours," he said, as they all went out one by one at the door, he himself holding it ajar and regarding them with a critical face as they passed, like a shepherd counting out his sheep. "You two counter-boys, keep your ears open

[1] carrier

to Michael's fingering, and don't ye go straying into the treble part along o' Dick and his set, as ye did last year; and mind this especially when we be in 'Arise, and hail.' Billy Chimlen, don't you sing quite so raving mad as you fain would; and, all o' ye, whatever ye do, keep from making a great scuffle on the ground, when we go in at people's gates; but go quietly, so as to strik' up all of a sudden, like spirits.''

"Farmer Ledlow's first?''

"Farmer Ledlow's first; the rest as usual.''

"And, Voss,'' said the tranter terminatively, "you keep house here till about half-past two; then heat the metheglin and cider in the warmer you'll find turned up upon the copper; and bring it wi' the victuals to church porch, as th'st know.''

Just before the clock struck twelve, they lighted the lanterns and started. The moon, in her third quarter, had risen since the snow-storm; but the dense accumulation of snow-cloud weakened her power to a faint twilight, which was rather pervasive of the landscape than traceable to the sky. The breeze had gone down, and the rustle of their feet, and tones of their speech, echoed with an alert rebound from every post, boundary-stone, and ancient wall they passed, even where the distance of the echo's origin was less than a few yards. Beyond their own slight noises nothing was to be heard, save the occasional howl of foxes in the direction of Yalbury Wood, or the brush of a rabbit among the grass now and then, as it scampered out of their way.

Most of the outlying homesteads and hamlets had been visited by about two o'clock; they then passed across the Home Plantation towards the main village. Pursuing no recognized track, great care was necessary in walking lest their faces should come in contact with the low-hanging boughs of the old trees, which in many spots formed dense overgrowths of interlaced branches.

"Times have changed from the times they used to be,'' said Mail, regarding nobody can tell what interesting old panoramas with an inward eye, and letting his outward glance rest on the ground, because it was as convenient a position as any. "People don't care much about us now! I've been thinking, we must be almost the last left in the county of the old string players. Barrel-organs, and they next door to 'em that you blow wi' your foot, have come in terribly of late years.''

"Ah!'' said Bowman, shaking his head; and old William, on seeing him, did the same thing.

"More's the pity,'' replied another. "Time was—long and merry ago now!— when not one of the varmits was to be heard of; but it served some of the choirs right. They should have stuck to strings as we did, and keep out clar'nets, and done away with serpents.[1] If you'd thrive in musical religion, stick to strings, says I.''

"Strings are well enough, as far as that goes,'' said Mr Spinks.

"There's worse things than serpents,'' said Mr Penny. "Old things pass away,

[1] early wind instrument

'tis true; but a serpent was a good old note: a deep rich note was the serpent.''

"Clar'nets, however, be bad at all times," said Michael Mail. "One Christmas—years agone now, years—I went the rounds wi' the Dibbeach choir. 'Twas a hard frosty night, and the keys of all the clar'nets froze—ah, they did freeze!—so that 'twas like drawing a cork every time a key was opened; the players o' 'em had to

go into a hedger and ditcher's chimley-corner, and thaw their clar'nets every now and then. An icicle o' spet hung down from the end of every man's clar'net, a span long; and as to fingers—well, there, if ye'll believe me, we had no fingers at all, to our knowledge."

"I can well bring back to my mind," said Mr Penny, "what I said to poor Joseph Ryme (who took the tribble part in High-Story Church for two-and-forty years) when they thought of having clar'nets there. 'Joseph,' I said, says I, 'depend upon't, if so be you have them tooting clar'nets you'll spoil the whole set-out. Clar'nets were not made for the service of Providence; you can see it by looking at 'em,' I said. And what cam o't? Why, my dear souls, the parson set up a barrel-organ on his own account within two years o' the time I spoke, and the old choir went to nothing."

"As far as look is concerned," said the tranter, "I don't for my part see that a fiddle is much nearer heaven than a clar'net. 'Tis farther off. There's always a rakish, scampish countenance about a fiddle that seems to say the Wicked One had a hand in making o'en; while angels be supposed to play clar'nets in heaven, or som'at like 'em, if ye may believe picters."

"Robert Penny, you were in the right," broke in the eldest Dewy. "They should ha' stuck to strings. Your brass-man, is brass—well and good; your reed-man, is reed—well and good; your percussion-man, is percussion—good again. But I don't care who hears me say it, nothing will speak to your heart wi' the sweetness of the man of strings!"

"Strings for ever!" said little Jimmy.

"Strings alone would have held their ground against all the newcomers in creation." ("True, true!" said Bowman.) "But clar'nets was death." ("Death they was!" said Mr Penny.) "And harmoniums," William continued in a louder voice, and getting excited by these signs of approval, "harmoniums and barrel-organs" ("Ah!" and groans from Spinks) "be miserable—what shall I call 'em—miserable—"

"Sinners," suggested Jimmy, who made large strides like the men, and did not lag behind like the other little boys.

"Miserable machines for such a divine thing as music!"

"Right, William, and so they be!" said the choir with earnest unanimity.

By this time they were crossing to a wicket in the direction of the school, which, standing on a slight eminence on the opposite side of a cross lane, now rose in unvarying and dark flatness against the sky. The instruments were returned, and all the band entered the enclosure, enjoined by old William to keep upon the grass.

"Number seventy-eight," he softly gave out as they formed round in a semicircle, the boys opening the lanterns to get a clearer light, and directing their rays on the books.

Then passed forth into the quiet night an ancient and well-worn hymn, embodying Christianity in words peculiarly befitting the simple and honest hearts of the quaint characters who sang them so earnestly.

> *Remember Adam's fall,*
>   *O thou man;*
> *Remember Adam's fall*
>   *From Heaven to Hell.*
> *Remember Adam's fall;*
> *How he hath condemn'd all*
> *In Hell perpetual*
>   *Therefore to dwell.*

> *Remember God's goodnesse,*
>   *O thou man:*
> *Remember God's goodnesse,*
>   *His promise made.*
> *Remember God's goodnesse;*
> *He sent His son sinlesse*
> *Our ails for to redress,*
>   *Our hearts to aid.*

> *In Bethlehem He was born,*
>   *O thou man:*
> *In Bethlehem He was born,*
>   *For mankind's sake.*
> *In Bethlehem He was born,*
> *Christmas Day i' the morn:*
> *Our Saviour did not scorn*
>   *Our faults to take.*

Give thanks to God alway,
O thou man:
Give thanks to God alway
With heart-felt joy.
Give thanks to God alway
On this our joyful day:
Let all men sing and say,
Holy, Holy!

Having concluded the last note, they listened for a minute or two, but found that no sound issued from the school-house.

"Forty breaths, and then, 'O what unbounded goodness!' number fifty-nine," said William.

This was duly gone through, and no notice whatever seemed to be taken of the performance.

"Surely 'tisn't an empty house, as befell us in the year thirty-nine and forty-three!" said old Dewy, with much disappointment.

"Perhaps she's jist come from some noble city, and sneers at our doings," the tranter whispered.

"'Od rabbit her!" said Mr Penny, with an annihilating look at the corner of the school chimney, "I don't quite stomach her, if this is it. Your plain music well done is as worthy as your other sort done bad, a' b'lieve, souls; so say I."

"Forty breaths, and then the last," said the leader authoritatively. "'Rejoice, ye tenants of the earth,' number sixty-four."

At the close, waiting yet another minute, he said in a clear loud voice, as he had said in the village at that hour and season for the previous forty years:

"A Merry Christmas to ye!"

*A letter written by Samuel Taylor Coleridge to his periodical
"The Friend", while travelling in Northern Europe*

CUSTOMS ON CHRISTMAS EVE

THERE is a Christmas custom here which pleased and interested me. The children make little presents to their parents, and to each other, and the parents to their children. For three or four months before Christmas the girls are all busy, and the boys save up their pocket money to buy these presents. What the present is to be is cautiously kept secret; and the girls have a world of contrivances to conceal it—such as working when they are out on visits, and the others are not with them, getting up in the morning before daylight, etc. Then on the evening before Christmas Day, one of the parlours is lighted up by the children, into which the parents must not go; a great yew bough is fastened on the table at a little distance from the wall, a multitude of little tapers are fixed in the bough, but not so as to burn it till they are nearly consumed, and coloured paper, etc., hangs and flutters from the twigs. Under this bough the children lay out in great order the presents they mean for their parents, still concealing in their pockets what they intend for each other. Then the parents are introduced, and each presents his little gift; they then bring out the remainder one by one from their pockets, and present them with kisses and embraces. Where I witnessed this scene there were eight or nine children, and the eldest daughter and the mother wept aloud for joy and tenderness; and the tears ran down the face of the father, and he clasped all his children so tight to his breast, it seemed as if he did it to stifle the sob that was rising within it. I was very much affected. The shadow of the bough and its appendages on the wall, and arching over on the ceiling, made a pretty picture; and then the raptures of the very little ones, when at last the twigs and their needles began to take fire and snap—O it was a delight to them! On the next day (Christmas Day) in the great parlour, the parents lay out on the table the presents for the children; a scene of more sober joy succeeds; as on this day, after an old custom, the mother says privately to each of her daughters, and the father to his sons, that which he has observed most praiseworthy and that which was most faulty in their

conduct. Formerly, and still in all the smaller towns and villages throughout these parts, the presents were sent by all the parents to some one fellow, who in high buskins, a white robe, a mask, and an enormous flax wig, personates Knecht Rupert, i.e. the servant Rupert. On Christmas night he goes round to every house, and says that Jesus Christ, his master, sent him thither. The parents and elder children receive him with great pomp and reverence, while the little ones are most terribly frightened. He then inquires for the children, and, according to their characters which he hears from the parents, he gives them the intended presents, as if they came out of heaven from Jesus Christ. Or, if they should have been bad children, he gives the parents a rod, and, in the name of his Master, recommends them to use it frequently. About seven or eight years old the children are let into the secret and it is curious how faithfully they keep it.

A letter from Jonathan Swift

CHRISTMAS GREETINGS TO STELLA
AND REBECCA DINGLEY

London, December 24. 1710

YOU will have a merryer Christmas-Eve than we here. I went up to Court before church, and in one of the rooms, there being but little company, a fellow in a red coat without a sword came up to me, and after words of course, askt me how the ladies did. I askt, what ladies? He said, Mrs Dingley and Mrs Johnson: Very well, said I, when I heard from them last: And pray when came you from thence, sir? Said he, I never was in Ireland; and just at that word Lord Winchelsea comes up to me, and the man went off; as I went out I saw him again, and recollected him, it was Vedeau with a pox: I then went and made my apologies that my head was full of something I had to say to lord Winchelsea etc., and I askt after his wife, and so all was well . . . . When I came from church I went up to Court again, where sir Edmund Bacon told me the bad news from Spain, which you will hear before this reaches you; as we have it now we are undone there, and it was odd to see the whole countenances of the Court changed so in two hours. Lady Mountjoy carried me home to dinner, where I staid not long after, and came home early, and now am got to bed, for you must always write to your MDs[1] in bed, that's a maxim.

> Mr White and Mr Red,
> Write to MD when abed;
> Mr Black and Mr Brown,
> Write to MD when you're down;
> Mr Oak and Mr Willow,
> Write to MD on your pillow.

What's this? faith I smell fire; what can it be; this house has a thousand stinks in it. I think to leave it on Thursday, and lodge over the way. Faith I must rise, and look at my chimney, for the smell grows stronger; stay—I have been up, and in my room, and found all safe, only a mouse within the fender to warm himself,

[1] Swift's shorthand: MD – My Dear (Stella) or My Dears (Stella and Rebecca Dingley)
Presto and Pdfr – Swift himself

76

which I could not catch. I smelt nothing there, but now in my bedchamber I smell it again; I believe I have singed the woolen curtain, and that's all, though I cannot smoak it. Presto's plaguy silly tonight; an't he? Yes, and so he be. Ay, but if I should wake and see fire. Well; I'll venture; so good night etc.

25th. Pray, young women, if I write so much as this every day, how will this paper hold a fortnight's work, and answer one of yours into the bargain? You never think of this, but let me go on like a simpleton. I wish you a merry Christmas, and many, many a one with poor Presto at some pretty place . . . .

26th. By the lord Harry I shall be undone here with Christmas boxes. The rogues at the Coffee-house have raised their tax, every one giving a crown, and I gave mine for shame, besides a great many half-crowns to great men's porters etc. . . . .

27th. . . . O faith I dreamed mightily of MD last night; but so confused I can't tell a word. I have made Ford acquainted with Lewis, and today we dined together; in the evening I called at one or two neighbours, hoping to spend a Christmas evening; but none were at home, they were all gone to be merry with others. I have often observed this, That in merry times everybody is abroad: where the duce are they? So I went to the Coffee-house, and talkt with Mr Addison an hour, who at last remembered to give me two letters, which I can't answer tonight, nor tomorrow either. I have other things to do than to answer naughty girls, an old saying and true. . . . .

30th. Morning. The weather grows cold, you sauce-boxes. . . . I'll go rise, for my hands are starving while I write in bed.—
Night. . . . Well, but when shall we answer this letter N.8 of MD's? Not till next year, faith. . . . Pray, pray, Dingley, let me go sleep; pray, pray, Stella, let me go slumber, and put out my wax candle.

31st. Morning. It is now seven, and I have got a fire, but am writing a-bed in my bed-chamber. 'Tis not shaving-day, so I shall be ready to go before church to Mr St John, and tomorrow I will answer our MD's letter.

> Would you answer MD's letter,
> On New-year's-day you'll do it better;
> For when the year with MD 'gins,
> It without MD never lins.
(These proverbs have always old words in them; *lins* is leaves off.)
> But if on New-year you write nones,
> MD then will bang your bones.—

But Patrick says I must rise.——

Night. I was early this morning with secretary St John, and gave him a memorial to get the queen's letter for the First-Fruits, who has promised to do it in a very few days. He told me he had been with the Duke of Marlborough, who was lamenting his former steps in joining with the Whigs, and said he was worn out with age, fatigues, and misfortunes. I swear it pitied me; and I really think they will not do well in too much mortifying that man, although indeed it is his own fault. He is covetous as hell, and ambitious as the Prince of it: he would fain have been general for life, and has broken all endeavours for Peace, to keep his greatness and get money. . . .

January 1st, 1711. Morning. I wish my dearest pretty Dingley and Stella a happy new-year, and health, and mirth, and good stomachs, and Fr's company. Faith, I did not know how to write Fr. I wondered what was the matter; but now I remember I always write pdfr. Patrick wishes me a happy New-year, and desires I would rise, for it is a good fire, and faith 'tis cold. . . . perhaps tonight I may answer MD's letter; so good-morrow, my mistresses all, good-morrow.

> I wish you both a merry New-year,
> Roast beef, minced pyes, and good strong beer.
> And me a share of your good cheer.
> That I was there, or you were here,
> And you're a little saucy dear.——
> Good morrow again, dear sirrahs. . . .

CHRISTMAS IN CORNWALL

In other places they have snow
And holly berries in a row
And crowded shops and cellophane
And Waits who shiver in the lane.

In Cornwall on the festal day
The sun shines brightly on the spray
Driving in pale transparency
At grey-brown cliffs from blue-green sea.

I never dreamed, as snug we sat
With Christmas tree and paper hat,
And all the joys that children bring,
Of climes where Christmas comes like Spring.

Once it was well; but now it's done . . .
A Christmas feast set out for *one*?
It does no good to mourn the past
Or claim that family bonds should last.

So down to Cornwall I will go,
Where salt plumes on the west winds blow,
To celebrate the Day alone
With gulls and larks and foam and sun.

Rosalind Wade

From Alexei Remizov's "On a Field Azure", translated by
Beatrice Scott

OLYA

OLYA wrote well: she didn't make mistakes.

Olya always had full marks for Russian.

Her teacher, Natalya Vasil'evna, liked Olya because she always got her spelling right.

And why did she get her spelling right?

Olya set herself this question and invented explanations—and one reason seemed the most likely.

When she was still very small, Olya would not be able to get to sleep sometimes; she would lie in bed at night, awake, and to amuse herself she divided words up into syllables—

ko-ro-va

ta-rel-ka

med-ved'

"I expect I divided every single word up into syllables then in the night and that's why I spell every word right now."

And Olya would notice mistakes in anyone's writing.

Yet she was still only in the third form.

She was eleven years old.

II

The holidays were drawing near—it was Christmas time.

Olya was longing to go home: she was lodging in town but her thoughts were all over there in Vatagino.

Olya was waiting for someone to come and fetch her.

But no, Natasha Grigor'evna's brother came for her and the Grigor'evs lived only three versts from them, so Olya had a letter from her mother.

Natalya Ivanovna wrote that Yuri Vasil'evitch Grigor'ev would take Olya to Vatagino: she had asked him to do this.

Olya read the letter and noticed it had two mistakes.

"Two mistakes!"

Next morning Olya went to the High School to ask for her return ticket home.

But the headmistress gave her no ticket—she didn't want to let her go back home.

"I can't let you go with a strange young man! If you could give me some assurance such as a letter from your mother or your father that they allowed you to travel with him, then I would let you go."

And Olya's spirits fell.

The letter lay in her pocket: if she produced it, the headmistress would at once give her leave and she would be home tomorrow—just in time.

"But Mummy's letter has two spelling mistakes! The headmistress will notice that my mother has made two mistakes. No, not for anything!"

So she didn't show the letter.

And she was left without her holiday.

Olya returned to her boarding establishment—everyone was going home: a father came for one, a mother for another, a third had a letter.

Olya alone was left.

And Olya wept all day and all night and all the next day and night.

On Christmas Eve Olya's Aunt, Marya Petrovna, came and took Olya to her house: she had only just heard that they had not allowed Olya to go home.

And Olya cried away a whole day at her Aunt's: her eyes got red with weeping, and swollen, and her nose got red and swollen too.

But she kept crying.

"Well, but why didn't you show your letter?" Marya Petrovna said in agitation.

"It had—two mistakes."

And again as soon as she remembered their house—the Christmas tree lit up . . . their favourite Granny telling about the Magi, how the Magi travelled with the star, and each time it seemed to Olya that there were many Magi and all women, bearing the star in their hands and the star guiding them with its light!— as soon as she remembered she burst into tears.

III

On Christmas morning Alexander Pavlovich arrived: he had ridden post all night from Vatagino.

Olya flung herself into his arms—how near to her it all was, the heavy uniform coat of Nicholas I's reign, and her father's grey hair, which she could hardly reach as she jumped, and his eyes!—Olya squealed with joy!

Well, now they could go.

Without waiting for dinner they set off home.

Olya did not feel very well on the way—she couldn't stand the motion of the sledge!—she got worn out.

And towards the end it rocked her to sleep.

She woke because the horses had neighed loudly.

They were at the porch already.

In the window the Christmas tree blazed—

And in the porch stood Natalya Ivanovna, their favourite Granny, Nurse Fatevna—they were all standing waiting for Olya.

Olya jumped out—and there was another treat for her!—she asked for tea and tea was standing all ready with lemon jam.

"Mummy guessed what happened to me on the journey!" Olya drank tea from her favourite cup with lemon jam.

And the children from the neighbouring house came.

They ran playing about the Christmas tree a long time.

They were given a great many sweets and dainties.

But they made their favourite ones themselves: they burnt sugar over a candle and the result was toffees—they loved doing this and were only given permission very rarely—but what delicious toffees they were!

Olya's father, her mother and her Granny made the sign of the cross over her when she went to bed.

Her father said:

"Christ be with you!"

Her mother said:

"May your guardian angel shield you!"

And Granny whispered:

"Blessed be the Lord!"

And when Olya lay in bed under her favourite blanket, Nurse Fatevna was poking about in all the corners for something:

"We must light all the ikon lamps. Today the unclean spirit is malevolent: he is angered that Christ is born."

And as she passed she too made the sign of the cross over Olya.

And Olya fell fast asleep, intoning a happy song in her nose.

From Thomas Hardy's "Tess of the D'Urbervilles"
THE 'TIVITY HYMN

OH yes; there's nothing like a fiddle," said the dairyman. "Though I do think that bulls are more moved by a tune than cows—at least that's my experience. Once there was an aged man over at Mellstock—William Dewy by name—one of the family that used to do a good deal of business as tranters [1] over there, Jonathan, do ye mind?—I knowed the man by sight as well as I know my own brother, in a manner of speaking. Well, this man was a-coming home—along from a wedding where he had been playing his fiddle, one fine moonlight night, and for shortness' sake he took a cut across Forty-acres, a field lying that way, where a bull was out to grass. The bull seed William, and took after him, horns aground, begad; and though William runned his best, and hadn't *much* drink in him (considering 'twas a wedding, and the folks well off), he found he'd never reach the fence and get over it in time to save himself. Well, as a last thought, he pulled out his fiddle as he runned, and struck up a jig, turning to the bull and backing to the corner. The bull softened down, and stood still, looking hard at William Dewy, who fiddled on and on, till a sort of smile stole over the bull's face. But no sooner did William stop playing and turn to get over hedge than the bull would stop his smiling and lower his horns towards the seat of William's breeches. Well, William had to turn about and play on, willy-nilly; and 'twas only three o'clock in the world, and 'a knowed that nobody would come that way for hours, and he so leery and tired that 'a didn't know what to do. When he had scraped till about four o'clock he felt that he verily would have to give over soon, and he said to himself, 'There's only this last tune between me and eternal welfare. Heaven save me, or I'm a done man!' Well, then he called to mind how he'd seen the cattle kneel o' Christmas Eves in the dead o' night. It was not Christmas Eve then, but it came into his head to play a trick upon the bull. So he broke into the 'Tivity Hymn, just as at Christmas carol-singing; when, lo and behold, down went the bull on his bended knees, in his ignorance, just as if 'twere the true 'Tivity

[1] carrier

84

night and hour. As soon as his horned friend were down, William turned, clinked off like a long-dog, and jumped safe over hedge, before the praying bull had got on his feet again to take after him. William used to say that he'd seen a man look a fool a good many times, but never such a fool as that bull looked when he found his pious feelings had been played upon, and 'twas not Christmas Eve.''

From Dorothy Hartley's "Food in England"

BOAR'S HEAD

Hey! Hey! Hey! Hey!
Hey! Hey! Hey! Hey!
The Boar's head in hand I bring,
With garlands gay in carrying,
I pray you all with me to sing
Hey! Hey! Hey! Hey!
Hey! Hey! Hey! Hey!
Lords and Knights and Squires,
Parsons, priests and vicars,
The Boar's head is the first mess!
Hey! Hey! Hey! Hey!
The Boar's head is armed gay!
(Old Song)

"Ye Olde Boar's Head" may be bought, handsomely prepared, at provision stores in the Christmas season. When made of a wild boar it is always justifiably expensive, but the homely version was peasant fare down the centuries, and if your men like cold boiled bacon, rather highly spiced, and you think it worth the trouble, a pig's head makes a very imposing side dish at very small cost.

A very simple boar's head dish. Get the head split and prepared at the butcher's. It should be in two halves except for the jointing skin at the top. Eyes, ears, snout and all the bone at the back should be removed and the brains wrapped separately. When it reaches you, lay it down quite flat and soak it in running water for an hour, rubbing it with salt and leaving it overnight in a large tub of strong salt water.

Next day, drain, wipe dry, and rub it well with salt and saltpetre (in the proportion of 1 drm. of saltpetre to 1 oz. of salt), pickling spice, and black pepper, then lay it in a kit, or large earthenware basin, which it will soon fill with brine. Keep rubbing on the salt daily, turning and rubbing thoroughly for a week (you may have to use more salt according to the size).

At the end of a week or ten days take it up, drain, and you now have a piece of salt pork which could be plain boiled or baked; but if it is for Christmas fare, put the head to boil very gently with vegetable trimmings, a large bunch of sage, onion skins, marjoram, bay leaves and peppercorns. Let it simmer *till the bones are loose*, allow it to cool in the broth, then lift it from the pan, and pull out the bones carefully. Skin the tongue, replace it, and truss the hot meat into a good conical shape. Dust with a little pepper and a suspicion of powdered mace as you work. Tie very firmly into shape and leave overnight under a weight.

To make the glaze. Meanwhile, ears, bones, gristle, etc., should have been boiled with plenty of flavouring herbs and spice till very stiff. Add a tablespoonful of brown vinegar and a couple of crushed egg-shells (these give it a bright clearness), strain into a jar, and by the time the pig's head is cold the glaze should be solidified to a stiff brown jelly.

When the head is cold, brush the liquid glazing over it several times till smoothly coated. The last coating should be *poured over* and left to set.

Serve "hym" on a convenient carving board, laid on a clean, flat fir bough. Give "hym" split almond tusks, and whatever your artistic eye suggests of trimmings of golden cut lemon peel, cut vegetable stars, bright green parsley, or wrinkled black shiny prunes for eyes, and finish with a wreath of holly; stand alongside a bowl of mustard sauce. It carves best lengthwise, is a very savoury form of cold spiced bacon, and looks very handsome on the sideboard at Christmas.

From Thomas Love Peacock's "The Misfortunes of Elphin"
DRUID XMAS

THE period of the winter solstice had been always a great festival with the
northern nations, the commencement of the lengthening of the days being,
indeed, of all points in the circle of the year, that in which the inhabitants of
cold countries have most cause to rejoice. This great festival was anciently called
Yule; whether derived from the Gothic *Iola*, to make merry; or from the Celtic
Hiaul, the sun; or from the Danish and Swedish *Hiul*, signifying wheel or revolution,
December being *Hiul-Month*, or the month of return; or from the Cimbric word
Ol, which has the important signification of ALE, is too knotty a problem to be
settled here: but Yule had been long a great festival, with both Celts and Saxons,
and, with the change of religion, became the great festival of Christmas, retaining
most of its ancient characteristics while England was Merry England: a phrase
which must be a mirifical puzzle to any one who looks for the first time on its
present lugubrious inhabitants.

The mistletoe of the oak was gathered by the Druids with great ceremonies as
a symbol of the season. The mistletoe continued to be so gathered, and to be
suspended in halls and kitchens, if not in temples, implying an unlimited privilege
of kissing: which circumstance, probably, led a learned antiquary to opine that
it was the forbidden fruit.

The Druids, at this festival, made, in a capacious cauldron, a mystical brewage
of carefully-selected ingredients, full of occult virtues, which they kept from the
profane, and which was typical of the new year and of the transmigration of the
soul. The profane, in humble imitation, brewed a bowl of spiced ale, or wine,
throwing therein roasted crabs; the hissing of which, as they plunged, piping hot,
into the liquor, was heard with much unction at midwinter, as typical of the
conjunct benignant influences of fire and strong drink. The Saxons called this the
Wassail-bowl, and the brewage of it is reported to have been one of the charms
with which Rowena fascinated Vortigern.

King Arthur kept his Christmas so merrily, that the memory of it passed into
a proverb: "As merry as Christmas in Caer Lleon."

S. J. Perelman

WAITING FOR SANTY

A CHRISTMAS PLAYLET

(With a Bow to Mr Clifford Odets)

Scene: *The sweat-shop of S. Claus, a manufacturer of children's toys, on North Pole Street.*
Time: *The night before Christmas.*

At rise, seven gnomes, Rankin, Panken, Rivkin, Riskin, Ruskin, Briskin, and Praskin, are discovered working furiously to fill orders piling up at stage right. The whir of lathes, the hum of motors, and the hiss of drying lacquer are so deafening that at times the dialogue cannot be heard, which is very vexing if you vex easily. (Note: The parts of Rankin, Panken, Rivkin, Riskin, Ruskin, Briskin, and Praskin are interchangeable, and may be secured directly from your dealer or the factory.)

RISKIN *(filing a Meccano girder, bitterly)*—A parasite, a leech, a bloodsucker—altogether a five-star nogoodnick! Starvation wages we get so he can ride around in a red team with reindeers!

RUSKIN *(jeering)*—Hey, Karl Marx, whyn'tcha hire a hall?

RISKIN *(sneering)*—Scab! Stool pigeon! Company spy! *(They tangle and rain blows on each other. While waiting for these to dry, each returns to his respective task.)*

BRISKIN *(sadly, to Panken)*—All day long I'm painting "Snow Queen" on these Flexible Flyers and my little Irving lays in a cold tenement with the gout.

PANKEN—You said before it was the mumps.

BRISKIN *(with a fatalistic shrug)*—The mumps—the gout—go argue with City Hall.

PANKEN *(kindly passing him a bowl)*—Here, take a piece fruit.

BRISKIN *(chewing)*—It ain't bad, for wax fruit.

PANKEN *(with pride)*—I painted it myself.

BRISKIN *(rejecting the fruit)*—Ptoo! Slave psychology!

RIVKIN *(suddenly, half to himself, half to the Party)*—I got a belly full of stars, baby. You make me feel like I swallowed a Roman candle.

PRASKIN (curiously)—What's wrong with the kid?

RISKIN—What's wrong with all of us? The system! Two years he and Claus's daughter's been making googoo eyes behind the old man's back.

PRASKIN—So what?

RISKIN (scornfully)—So what? Economic determinism! What do you think the kid's name is—J. Pierpoint Rivkin? He ain't even got for a bottle Dr Brown's Celery Tonic. I tell you, it's like gall in my mouth two young people shouldn't have a room where they could make great music.

RANKIN (warningly)—Shhh! Here she comes now! (Stella Claus enters, carrying a portable phonograph. She and Rivkin embrace, place a record on the turntable, and begin a very slow waltz, unmindful that the phonograph is playing "Cohen on the Telephone".)

STELLA (dreamily)—Love me, sugar?

RIVKIN—I can't sleep, I can't eat, that's how I love you. You're a double malted with two scoops of whipped cream; you're the moon rising over Mosholu Parkway; you're a two weeks' vacation at Camp Nitgedaiget! I'd pull down the Chrysler Building to make a bobbie pin for your hair!

STELLA—I've got a stomach full of anguish. Oh, Rivvy, what'll we do?

PANKEN (*sympathetically*)—Here, try a piece fruit.

RIVKIN (*fiercely*)—Wax fruit—that's been my whole life! Imitations! Substitutes! Well, I'm through! Stella, tonight I'm telling your old man. He can't play mumblety-peg with two human beings! (*The tinkle of sleigh bells is heard offstage, followed by a voice shouting, "Whoa, Dasher! Whoa, Dancer!" A moment later S. Claus enters in a gust of mock snow. He is a pompous bourgeois of sixty-five who affects a white beard and a false air of benevolence. But tonight the ruddy color is missing from his cheeks, his step falters, and he moves heavily. The gnomes hastily replace the marzipan they have been filching.*)

STELLA (*anxiously*)—Papa! What did the specialist say to you?

CLAUS (*brokenly*)—The biggest professor in the country . . . the best cardiac man that money could buy . . . I tell you I was like a wild man.

STELLA—Pull yourself together, Sam!

CLAUS—It's no use. Adhesions, diabetes, sleeping sickness, decalcomania—oh, my God! I got to cut out climbing in chimneys, he says—me, Sanford Claus, the biggest toy concern in the world!

STELLA (*soothingly*)—After all, it's only one man's opinion.

CLAUS—No, no, he cooked my goose. I'm like a broken uke after a Yosian picnic. Rivkin!

RIVKIN—Yes, Sam.

CLAUS—My boy, I had my eye on you for a long time. You and Stella thought you were too foxy for an old man, didn't you? Well, let bygones be bygones. Stella, do you love this gnome?

STELLA (*simply*)—He's the whole stage show at the Music Hall, Papa; he's Toscanini conducting Beethoven's Fifth; he's—

CLAUS (*curtly*)—Enough already. Take him. From now on he's a partner in the firm. (*As all exclaim, Claus holds up his hand for silence.*) And tonight he can take my route and make the deliveries. It's the least I could do for my own flesh and blood. (*As the happy couple kiss, Claus wipes away a suspicious moisture and turns to the other gnomes.*) Boys, do you know what day tomorrow is?

GNOMES (*crowding around expectantly*)—Christmas!

CLAUS—Correct. When you look in your envelopes tonight, you'll find a little present from me—a forty per cent pay cut. And the first one who opens his trap—gets this. (*As he holds up a tear-gas bomb and beams at them, the gnomes utter cries of joy, join hands, and dance around him shouting exultantly. All except Riskin and Briskin, that is, who exchange a quick glance and go underground.*)

CURTAIN

PATAPAN

Willie, take your little drum,
With your whistle, Robin, come!
   When we hear the fife and drum,
Ture-lure-lu, pata-pata-pan,
    When we hear the fife and drum,
    Christmas should be frolicsome.

Thus the men of olden days
Loved the King of kings to praise:
   When they hear the fife and drum,
Ture-lure-lu, pata-pata-pan,
    When they hear the fife and drum,
    Sure our children won't be dumb!

God and man are now become
More at one than fife and drum.
   When you hear the fife and drum,
Ture-lure-lu, pata-pata-pan,
    When you hear the fife and drum,
    Dance, and make the village hum!

Anon

From Beatrix Potter's "The Tailor of Gloucester"

SIMPKIN'S CHRISTMAS

THE tailor lay ill for three days and nights; and then it was Christmas Eve, and very late at night. The moon climbed up over the roofs and chimneys, and looked over the gateway into College Court. There were no lights in the windows, nor any sound in the houses; all the city of Gloucester was fast asleep under the snow.

And still Simpkin wanted his mice, and mewed as he stood beside the four-post bed.

But it is the old story that all the beasts can talk, in the night between Christmas Eve and Christmas Day in the morning (though there are very few folk that can hear them, or know what it is that they say).

When the Cathedral clock struck twelve there was an answer—like an echo of the chimes—and Simpkin heard it, and came out of the tailor's door, and wandered about in the snow.

From all the roofs and gables and old wooden houses in Gloucester came a thousand merry voices singing the old Christmas rhymes—all the old songs that ever I heard of, and some that I don't know, like Whittington's bells.

First and loudest the cocks cried out—"Dame get up, and bake your pies!"

"Oh dilly, dilly, dilly!" sighed Simpkin.

And now in a garret there were lights and sounds of dancing, and cats came from over the way.

"Hey, diddle, diddle, the cat and the fiddle! All the cats in Gloucester—except me," said Simpkin.

Under the wooden eaves the starlings and sparrows sang of Christmas pies; the jack-daws woke-up in the Cathedral tower; and although it was the middle of the night the throstles and robins sang; the air was quite full of little twittering tunes.

But it was all rather provoking to poor hungry Simpkin!

Particularly he was vexed with some little shrill voices from behind a wooden lattice. I think that there were bats, because they always have very small voices—especially in a black forest, when they talk in their sleep, like the Tailor of Gloucester.

94

From Geoffrey Willans' "How to be Topp"

DING-DONG FARELY MERILY FOR XMAS

XMAS all grown ups sa is the season for the kiddies but this do not prevent them from taking a tot or 2 from the bot and having, it may seme, a beter time than us. For children in fact Xmas is often a bit of a strane wot with pretending that everything is a surprise. Above all father xmas is a strane. You canot so much as mention that there is no father xmas when some grown-sa Hush not in front of wee tim. So far as i am concerned if father xmas use langwage like that when he tripped over the bolster last time we had beter get a replacement.

CHRISTMAS EVE

Hurra for Xmas Eve wot a scurrying there was in the molesworth household. First of all mr molesworth issued jovially with the hammer to hang the decorations – red white purple streemers holly mistletoe lights candles snow Mery Xmas All: mrs molesworth is in the kitchen with the mince pies, all rosy and shining: and judge of the excitement of the 2 boys!

In fact, it is a proper SHAMBLES.

Pop drop the hamer on the cat in the kitchen the xmas puding xplode with a huge crash and the cat spring up the curtains. Outside the sno lie deep and crisp and ect. and just as pop fall off the steplader the WATES arive.

WATES are 3 litle gurls with a torch who go as folows:

> HEE HEE HEE NOEL NOEL GO ON GURT
> NO-ELL NO-ELL NO YOU RING the KING of IS-RAY-ER-ELL.
> PING! PING!
> TANNER FOR THE WATES, PLEASE.

This of course is money for jam but grown ups are so intoxicated with xmas they produce a shiling. Imagine a whole weeks poket money just for that when you can get it all on the wireless anyway if you want it. Or whether you want it or not.

molesworth 2 is very amusing about carols i must sa he hav a famous carol

> *While shepherds washed their socks by night*
> *All seated on the ground*
> *A bar of sunlight soap came down ect.*

He think this is so funy he roar with larffter whenever he think of it and as he
spend most of the night thinking of it i do not get much slepe chiz. i sa SHUTUP
molesworth 2 SHUTUP i want to go to slepe but in vain the horid zany go cakling
on. It is not as if it is funy i mean a bar of sunlight soap ha-ha well it is not ha-ha-
ha-ha a bar of ha-ha-ha-ha . . .

Oh well.

Another thing about xmas eve is that your pater always reads the xmas carol by
c. dickens. You canot stop this aktually although he pretend to ask you whether
you would like it. He sa:

Would you like me to read the xmas carol as it is xmas eve, boys?

We are listening to the space serial on the wireless, daddy.

But you canot prefer that nonsense to the classick c. dickens?

Be quiet. He is out of control and heading for jupiter.

But

He's had it the treen space ships are ataking him ur-ur-ur-*whoosh*. Out of control
limping in the space vacuum for evermore unless they can get the gastric fuel
compressor tampons open.

I—

Why don't they try Earth on the intercom? They will never open those tampons
with only a z-ray griper. They will—

Father thwarted strike both boys heavily with loaded xmas stoking and tie
their hands behind their backs. He cart them senseless into the sitting room and
prop both on his knees. Then he begin:

THE XMAS CAROL by C. DICKENS
(published by grabber and grabber)

Then he rub hands together and sa You will enjoy this boys it is all about ghosts
and goodwill. It is tip-top stuff and there is an old man called scrooge who hates
xmas and canot understand why everyone is so mery. To this you sa nothing except
that scrooge is your favourite character in fiction next to tarzan of the apes. But
you can sa anything chiz. Nothing in the world in space is ever going to stop those
fatal words:

Marley was dead

Personaly i do not care a d. whether Marley was dead or not it is just that there
is something about the xmas Carol which makes paters and grown ups read with
grate XPRESION, and this is very embarassing for all. It is all right for the first
part they just roll the r's a lot but wate till they come to scrooge's nephew. When
he sa Mery Christmas uncle it is like an H-bomb xplosion and so it go on until
you get to Tiny Tim chiz chiz chiz he is a weed. When Tiny Tim sa God bless us
every one your pater is so overcome be burst out blubbing. By this time boys hav
bitten through their ropes and make good their escape so 900000000 boos to
bob cratchit.

XMAS NITE

At last the tiny felows are tucked up snug in their beds with 3 pilow slips awaiting santa claus. As the lite go off a horid doubt assale the mind e.g. suposing there *is* a santa claus. Zoom about and lay a few traps for him.

Determin to lie awake and get him but go to slepe in the end chiz and dream of space ships. While thus employed something do seem to be hapning among the earthmen.

CRASH!

Be quiet you will wake them up. Hav you got the mecano his is the one with 3 oranges if you drop that pedal car agane i shall scream where are the spangles can you not tie a knot for heavens sake ect. ect.

It would seem that the earthmen are up to something but you are far to busy with the treens who are defending the space palace with germ guns. So snore on, fair child, snore on with thy inocent dreams and do not get the blud all over you.

THE DAY

Xmas day always start badly becos molesworth 2 blub he hav not got the reel rools-royce he asked for. We then hav argument that each hav more presents than the other. A Mery Xmas everybode sa scrooge in the end but we just call each other clot-faced wets so are you you you you pointing with our horny fingers it is very joly i must sa. In the end i wear molesworth 2's cowboy suit and he pla with my air gun so all is quiet.

Then comes DINNER.

This is super as there are turkey crackers nuts cream plum puding jely and everything. We wash it down with a litle ginger ale but grown ups all drink wine ugh and this make all the old lades and grans very sprightly i must sa. They sa how sweet we are they must be dotty until pater raps the table and look v. solemn. He holds up his glass and sa in a low voice.

The QUEEN. Cheers cheers cheers for the queen we all drink and hurra for england.

Then pater sa in much lower voice ABSENT FRIENDS and everyone else sa absent friends absent friends absent friends ect. and begin blubbing. In fact it do not seme that you can go far at xmas time without blubbing of some sort and when they listen to the wireless in the afternoon all about the lonely shepherd and the lighthousemen they are in floods of tears.

Still xmas is a good time with all those presents and good food and i hope it will never die out or at any rate not until i am grown up and hav to pay for it all. So ho skip and away the next thing we shall be taken to peter pan for a treat so brace up brace up.

I SING OF A MAIDEN

I sing of a maiden
   That is makèles,
King of all kinges
   To her sone she ches.[1]

He cam also stille
   There his moder was,
As dew in Aprille
   That falleth on the grass.

He cam also stille
   To his moderes bour,
As dew in Aprille
That falleth on the flour.

He cam also stille
   There his moder lay,
As dew in Aprille
   That falleth on the spray.

Moder and maiden
   Was never non but sche;
Well may swich a lady
   Godès moder be.

Anon

[1] chose

STAR OF THE NATIVITY

It was wintertime.
The wind blew hard from the plain.
And the infant was cold in the cave
On the slope of a hill.
He was warmed by the breath of an ox.
The cattle huddled
Within the cave.
A warm mist drifted over the manger.

On a cliff afar the shepherds, awake,
Shook off the wisps of straw
And hayseed of their beds,
And sleepily gazed in the vastness of night.

They beheld the fields in drifted snows,
Gravestones and fences,
The shafts of a cart,
And a sky of stars above the graveyard;

And near them, unseen until then,
Like a watchman's candle
One star alone and shy
That shone on the road to Bethlehem.

At times it looked like a hayrick aflame,
Apart from God and the sky;
Like a barn on fire,
Like a farmstead ablaze in the night.

It reared in the sky like a flaming stack
Of straw and hay,
In the midst of a Creation
Amazed by this new star in the world.

And the flame grew steadily wider, .
Large as a portent.
Then three stargazers
Hastened to follow the marvellous light.

Behind them, their camels with gifts.
Their caparisoned asses, each one smaller
In size, came daintily down the hillside.

And all new matters that were to come after
Arose as a vision of wonder in space.
All thoughts of ages, all dreams, new worlds,
All the future of galleries and of museums,
All the games of fairies, works of inventors,
And the yule trees, and the dreams all children dream:
The tremulous glow of candles in rows,
The gold and silver of angels and globes
(A wind blew, raging, long from the plain),
And the splendour of tinsel and toys under trees.

A part of the pond lay hidden by alders;
A part could be seen afar from the cliff
Where rocks were nesting among the treetops.
The shepherds could see each ass and camel
Trudging its way by the water mill.
''Let us go and worship the miracle,''
They said, and belted their sheepskin coats.

Their bodies grew warm, walking through snows.
There were footprints that glinted like mica
Across bright fields, on the way to the inn.
But the dogs on seeing the tracks in starshine
Growled loud in anger as if at a flame.

The frosty night was like a fairy tale.
And phantoms from mountain ridges in snows
Invisibly came to walk in the crowd.
The dogs grew fearful of ghosts around
And huddled beside the shepherd lads.

Across these valleys and mountain roads,
Unbodied, unseen by mortal eyes,
A heavenly host appeared in the throng,
And each footprint gleamed as an angel's foot.

At dawn the cedars lifted their heads.
A multitude gathered around the cave.
"Who are ye?" said Mary. They spoke: "We come
As shepherds of flocks, as envoys of heaven;
In praise of the Child and thy glory we come."
"The cave is too crowded. Abide ye a while."

Before dawnlight, in gloom, in ashen dark,
The drivers and shepherds stamped in the cold.
The footmen quarrelled with mounted men;
Beside the well and the water trough
The asses brayed and the camels bellowed.

The dawn! It swept the last of the stars
Like grains of dust from the vaulted sky.
Then Mary allowed the Magi alone
To enter the cleft of the mountainside.

He slept in His manger in radiant light
As a moonbeam sleeps in a hollow tree.
The breath of the ox and the ass kept warm
His hands and feet in the cold of night.

The Magi remained in the twilight cave;
They whispered softly, groping for words.
Then someone in darkness touched the arm
Of one near the manger, to move him aside;
Behold, like a guest above the threshold,
The Star of Nativity gazed on the Maid.

Boris Pasternak, translated by Eugene M. Kayden

102

A CHRISTMAS CAROL

Before the paling of the stars,
    Before the winter morn,
    Before the earliest cockcrow
Jesus Christ was born;
        Born in a stable,
    Cradled in a manger,
In the world His hands had made
        Born a stranger.

Priest and King lay fast asleep
    In Jerusalem,
Young and old lay fast asleep
    In crowded Bethlehem;
Saint and Angel, ox and ass,
    Kept a watch together,
    Before the Christmas daybreak
    In the winter weather.

Jesus on His Mother's breast
    In the stable cold,
Spotless Lamb of God was He,
    Shepherd of the fold:
Let us kneel with Mary Maid,
    With Joseph bent and hoary,
With Saint and Angel, ox and ass,
    To hail the King of glory.

Christina Rossetti

From Natala de la Fere's "Italian Bouquet"

THE MOUNTAINS OF PAPA MORELLI

"WILL you come with me to the Piazza Navona, Signora?" asked Papa Morelli one evening a week before Christmas.

"Gladly," I replied, "but why especially the Piazza Navona?"

"I know . . . another figure," suggested his twelve-year-old daughter Maria Grazia.

"Yes, I expect that's it—another figure," agreed his older daughter Teresa.

Signora Morelli said nothing but slowly nodded her head in silence.

"Another figure?" I queried with curiosity.

"Yes of course, they know," explained Papa Morelli seriously. "Every year another figure is added to our crib at Christmas and I am the one who must choose it in the market for Christmas figures in the Piazza Navona."

"But why so especially there?" I asked in my unpardonable ignorance.

"Why?" repeated Signora Morelli, amazed, "because that is where they have the special market every year for figures and everything else for Christmas cribs."

"Why don't you buy the mountains this year, babbo?" asked Maria Grazia with what I thought was an exaggeratedly casual air.

"Yes, haven't we enough figures?" went on Teresa. (Did I imagine a quick sidelong look at her mother?) "We must have more than thirty figures now."

Papa Morelli did not answer, it was as if he had not heard. It was his wife who answered loyally:

"Your father will buy the mountains when he is ready, and not before."

But I thought I detected a note of resignation in her voice. And when he glanced at her somewhat sheepishly, the mystery of the mountains seemed real enough to me. Quietly he got up and said, "Shall we go now, Signora?"

I jumped up with alacrity, partly to dispel what I felt sure was an "atmosphere", even if only a light one, and partly because I really was eager to see this market which sounded quite unique.

In the crowded bus we did not have a chance to speak, so I let my mind dwell affectionately on this little family, so simple, united and open-hearted and so kind to have invited me to spend my first Christmas in Rome with them.

The Piazza Navona is one of the oldest squares in Rome and so well hidden by a maze of narrow little streets that if you do not know about it you could live in the city almost indefinitely without ever seeing it. Actually it is not a square, but a long rectangle with a fabulous Bernini fountain in the centre and two others, less grandiose, at either end. Completely surrounded by houses that have remained unchanged for centuries, it is unlike any other square in Rome. And the week before Christmas, unlike any other square in the world.

When Papa Morelli and I emerged from one of the tiny streets into the piazza,

I could only stand and marvel. Both its sides were tightly lined with stalls, peopled by a multitude of miniatures. Thousands of figures of the Virgin Mary, Saint Joseph, the Infant Jesus, shepherds, kings, peasants, asses, oxen, camels and sheep arranged in groups or in processions or just jumbled anyhow, stretched right down to the far end. Music blared forth from loudspeakers; sweet stalls where the traditional nougat was made and sold in slabs up to almost any length and weight, did a roaring trade. The nougat was the only merchandise allowed to be sold apart from the figures.

Carefully, lovingly and beautifully made, either in wood or plaster, these saintly biblical characters quietly knelt, sat or stood in silent testimony to the greatest event in the history of man. Hanging all around them were replicas, big and small, of the holy stable; glittering Stars of Bethlehem and comets swung on high and range after range of papier mâché painted mountains completed the décor. Every stall was arranged according to the individual taste of its owner and some of the effects were dramatic and imposing. The noise and gaiety increased as the square became more and more crowded. Children stood wide-eyed pointing to the figures they wanted their parents to buy for the crib at home.

Papa Morelli pulled my arm gently. ''Why so silent, Signora? You haven't spoken a word since we came.''

How could I explain the deep impression made upon me by myriads of figures so beautifully fashioned and so dignified in their attitudes of mute adoration? It seemed

105

almost sacrilegious to watch them being bought for a few lire, wrapped up in newspaper and thrust into baskets by the milling, shouting throng which then crowded round the nougat stalls to complete traditional Christmas purchases.

"Which one are you going to buy this year?" I asked Papa Morelli, at last.

We walked along inspecting each stall carefully.

"I have all the principal ones," he said. "The Virgin, St Joseph, the Child, of course, the Three Kings and some shepherds, but I need a few peasants . . . yes, I think that peasant woman in her wide red skirt and the man over there kneeling, holding a sheep."

"Are they the right size?" I asked.

"Oh yes, about ten centimetres . . . yes, they'll match the others nicely."

We bought them and he stuffed them in his pockets.

"There," he said happily, "they will just fill that empty corner in front nicely."

I longed to offer to buy some mountains for his crib, but remembering the mysterious "atmosphere" earlier in the evening when they had been mentioned, I refrained and, as events turned out, I did not know whether to be glad or sorry for having held back.

As we were turning away to go to the near-by nougat stall I was struck by the figure of a tiny Madonna holding the Child. She was not looking down at Him in the usual way but upwards, as if to thank God in His Heaven for this wondrous miracle. She was carved out of wood, and her delicate colouring and ecstatic expression enhanced by the soft light of a paper-covered bulb so captivated me that I did not hesitate for a second. I bought her, handing over my lire quickly with a curious sense of shame for the inglorious gesture, and snatched her out of reach of the proffered sheet of newspaper. Slipping the carving inside my coat, I held it against my heart for the rest of the evening.

Two days before Christmas Papa Morelli came home from the office with a busy air and shut himself in the front room with a request that he was not to be disturbed. The family and I had supper in the kitchen and his was kept warm in the oven.

"Well . . . it's Christmas again," sighed the Signora.

"And the crib," sighed Maria Grazia.

"And the crib," echoed Teresa hopelessly.

Tentatively I tried to discover why the making of the Christmas crib should cast such a gloom over this happy household every year.

"It'll begin soon now," said Signora Morelli softly, towards ten o'clock.

Just as I was about to ask some indiscreet questions, we heard the key turn in the lock and Papa Morelli crossed the hall and came in with a broad, satisfied smile.

"My love," he turned to his wife with a courtly gesture, "you will be the first to see it."

Signora Morelli rose calmly and with a significant look at all of us left the room with her husband.

"What is behind all this?" I asked Teresa, throwing discretion to the winds.

"It's the mountains," she explained, "every year it's the mountains."

"And it'll be the same again this year, you'll see," said Maria Grazia slowly.

"What's the matter with the mountains?" I asked bluntly.

"We don't know – yet."

"Last year they were too high."

"And the year before that they were too low."

"And I remember one year when they looked more like a stormy sea than mountains."

"He will make them himself," went on Maria Grazia, "he loves making them. He collects stiff brown paper for weeks beforehand and we always have such a mess of paint to clear up afterwards."

"But the real trouble is Mother, she can never stop herself saying what she thinks of the mountains, and it's always wrong. Then there's an awful row— you'll see."

"That's the trouble," Teresa explained further. "If only Mother would let him do what he likes with his mountains and admire them whatever they look like."

In a few moments their worst forebodings were confirmed. Voices raised in argument came from the closed room, Papa Morelli's in a sharp, gradual crescendo, and Signora Morelli's in shrill and excited trills. The girls looked at each other and then at me. Then they sat hunched up waiting for the eruption. It came inevitably. The door opposite was flung open and then slammed. Signora Morelli burst into the kitchen very pink-cheeked.

"They are too dark, I said so because they are. How can I say what isn't true? They are too dark!"

Once more we heard the key turned deliberately in the lock of the front room door. Teresa got up resignedly and turned off the oven. Signora Morelli slept with the girls that night.

The next evening was Christmas Eve. Nobody had seen Papa Morelli since the day before, but we heard him returning from the office very early. He stumped down the corridor and then, after much grunting and heaving, went back to the front room staggering under the burden of the large linen cupboard door. He had heaved it off its hinges leaving the shelves of linen exposed to public view. Then he locked himself in again.

The rest of us passed the time quietly playing cards in the kitchen. Supper time came and went.

"He'll come out just before it's time to go to midnight Mass, I suppose," said Signora Morelli.

"Hasn't he had anything to eat since yesterday?" I enquired anxiously.

"Of course," she laughed. "I heard him come in here very late in the night, and this morning I saw he'd eaten up everything. He go hungry!"

About an hour later the door opened and we all concentrated very hard on our cards.

"Signora," he said quietly.

I looked up feigning surprise.

"Me, Signore?"

"Certainly, Signora, as our guest I want you to be the first to see my crib."

As I went with him the family gave me encouraging looks and nods.

A moment later I stood facing a virtual work of art. Papa Morelli had used the linen cupboard door as a base supported by trestles. On it he had designed and built a corner of the Bethlehem countryside. Sparse tufts of grass and stony patches through which twisted paths led up to the stable were realistically reproduced in paper and cardboard truthfully painted, and perfectly arranged in natural disorder. Peasants standing at the doors of their huts with their animals grazing or resting near by, filled the foreground. The steep, narrow paths all converged upon the stable. The Three Kings leading their laden camels were resplendent in brilliant costumes and head-dresses, while simple shepherds knelt in prayer surrounded by their sheep. Inside the dim stable I could discern the shadowy ox and ass. Saint Joseph in an attitude of devout humility was bending over the Virgin in her blue mantle, seated in the centre looking at her empty arms.

"The Child is not born yet," whispered Papa Morelli softly. "He will be put in her arms when we come back from Mass."

I raised my eyes to the glittering tinsel star of Bethlehem shining over the stable roof. Rising in sombre, majestic splendour along the whole background were the dark—the "too dark"—mountains. Only, for me they were not too dark.

"Papa Morelli," I said softly, "it is one of the loveliest things I have ever seen. It is perfect."

He pressed my hand. "And the mountains, Signora, are they too dark?"

I wished he had not asked me that. I did not want to upset Signora Morelli any more than I wanted to hurt him. I hesitated. He himself saved me from my dilemma.

"How can they be too dark when I have little lights hidden everywhere to light it all up? It's the first year I've had them, and you'll see what a wonderful surprise it will be." He came closer and whispered in my ear. "They don't know."

He went to the door and shouted:

"Well? Are you coming to see the crib or aren't you?"

They filed into the room obediently and with quiet, serious expressions gazed on the masterpiece. Then, suddenly, Papa Morelli re-established a true, happy Christmas Eve. He put his arms round his wife and kissed her. "Tell me it is beautiful, tesoro . . . my treasure. Just say it for me, and then I shall show you how light the mountains really are."

She laughed happily and stroked his cheek. "Why, of course, Gino, of course it's beautiful, you shouldn't listen to me."

"Ah, but you were right then, darling, quite right, it was I who would not admit it, but watch now!"

He stepped to the switch in the wainscoting and bent down. "Now you will see your light mountains," he pronounced proudly.

He turned on the switch and—we were in complete darkness. Every light in the apartment had fused. For a moment there was a bitter silence.

"Santa Madonna," he wailed, "Santa Madonna, now look what I've done!"

Immediately we all rallied to his aid.

"Why, it's nothing, nothing at all, only a little fuse that can be put right in no time," I cried.

"Gino, I'm sure it's wonderful all lit up," his wife encouraged him, "we'll get it fixed quickly before it's time to go to Mass. Teresa, go and find the candle . . . Maria Grazia, get some matches . . . I'll get the step-ladder."

We all sprang into action, feeling our way in the dark. Bumping and jostling each other, we scrambled about in the kitchen opening cupboards and drawers, fumbling badly in our haste to help him remedy the situation and enjoy his triumph.

"What can have gone wrong?" we heard him muttering to himself all alone in the dark front room.

"Don't worry, don't get excited," Signora Morelli called out to him. "We are finding everything, just one minute more, tesoro."

At last the candle was lit, the step-ladder fixed under the fuse-box and the candle held on high to light his way. He climbed up and fiddled for what seemed an endless time. Then, with a relieved "finalmente", he clambered down and we switched on the light in the hall. Tactfully we left him alone to readjust his precious wires, rushing in in a body as he shouted a triumphant, "Ecco! Done!"

Now, in the surrounding darkness, the little holy scene lay revealed in dramatic light and shade; the figures cast life-like shadows and had they really moved I don't think I would have been surprised; the Star of Bethlehem shone like a real star and the still childless Virgin sat serenely in a golden aura. The glorious moment was at hand.

When we returned from Mass, Papa Morelli laid the Child reverently in His mother's arms, and a little later we went to our rooms to sleep with His message of peace and goodwill in our hearts.

CHRISTMAS LANDSCAPE

Tonight the wind gnaws
with teeth of glass,
the jackdaw shivers
in caged branches of iron,
the stars have talons.

There is hunger in the mouth
of vole and badger,
silver agonies of breath
in the nostril of the fox,
ice on the rabbit's paw.

Tonight has no moon,
no food for the pilgrim;
the fruit tree is bare,
the rose bush a thorn
and the ground bitter with stones.

But the mole sleeps, and the hedgehog
lies curled in a womb of leaves,
the bean and the wheat-seed
hug their germs in the earth
and the stream moves under the ice.

Tonight there is no moon,
but a new star opens
like a silver trumpet over the dead.
Tonight in a nest of ruins
the blessed babe is laid.

And the fir tree warms to a bloom of candles,
the child lights his lantern,
stares at his tinselled toy;
our hearts and hearths
smoulder with live ashes.

In the blood of our grief
the cold earth is suckled,
in our agony the womb
convulses its seed,
in the cry of anguish
the child's first breath is born.

Laurie Lee

112

WINTER'S SNOW

E. Caswall

R. O. Morris

SOLO
Moderato

VOICE

1. See a - mid the win-ter's snow, Born for us on_ earth be - low;
2. Lo, with - in a man-ger lies He who built the_ star - ry skies;

ACCPT.

See the ten - der Lamb ap - pears, Pro-mised from e - ter - nal years:
He who, throned in height sub - lime, Sits a - mid the_ che - ru - bim:

CHORUS

S.
A.

Hail, thou ev - er - bless - ed_ morn; Hail, re-demp-tion's hap - py dawn;_

T.
B.

(Accpt. ad lib.)

Sing through all Je - ru - sa - lem, — Christ is born in — Beth- le - hem.

3 Say, ye holy shepherds, say
What your joyful news to-day;
Wherefore have ye left your sheep
On the lonely mountain steep?

Hail, thou ever-blessed morn; etc.

4 'As we watched at dead of night,
Lo, we saw a wondrous light;
Angels singing "Peace on earth"
Told us of the Saviour's birth':

Hail, thou ever-blessed morn; etc.

5 Sacred infant, all divine,
What a tender love was thine,
Thus to come from highest bliss
Down to such a world as this:

Hail, thou ever-blessed morn; etc.

6 Teach, O teach us, holy Child,
By thy face so meek and mild,
Teach us to resemble thee,
In thy sweet humility:

Hail, thou ever-blessed morn; etc.

COVENTRY CAROL

Pageant of the Shearmen
and Tailors, 15th century

Original version of 1591

SOPRANO

Lul - ly, lul - la, thou lit - tle tiny child, By by, lul - ly lul -

TENOR
BASS

-lay, thou lit - tle tiny child, By by, lul - ly lul - lay.

1. O sis - ters too, How may we do For to pre - serve this day This
2. He - rod, the king, In his rag - ing, Char - ged he hath this day His
3. That woe is me, Poor child for thee! And e - ver morn and day, For

poor young-ling, For whom we do sing, By by, lul - ly lul - lay?
men of might, In his own sight, All young chil - dren to slay.
thy part- ing Neither say nor sing By by, lul - ly lul - lay!

HERRICK'S CAROL

Robert Herrick (1647)

German
Arr. Martin Shaw

Rather quick

SOPRANO
ALTO

1. What swee-ter mu - sic can we bring___ Than a ca - rol,
2. Dark and dull night, fly hence a - way, And give the hon - our

TENOR
BASS

The birth of this our
That sees De - cem - ber

for to___ sing The birth of this our heav'n - ly___ King? A -
to this___ day, That sees De - cem - ber turned to___ May, If

(Melody in Tenor)

A -
If

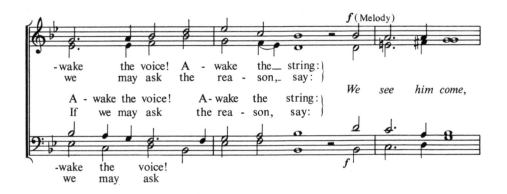

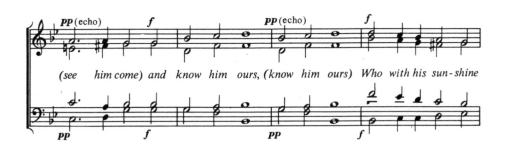

3 The darling of the world is come,
  And fit it is we find a room
  To welcome him. The nobler part
  Of all the house here is the heart:

    We see him come, etc.

4 Which we will give him, and bequeath
  This holly and this ivy wreath,
  To do him honour who's our King,
  And Lord of all this revelling:

    We see him come, etc.

IN DULCI JUBILO

Tr. Percy Dearmer

German, 14th century
(harm. Bartholomew Gesius, 1601)

VERSES 1, 2, & 3
Allegro

SOPRANO
ALTO

TENOR
BASS

1. In dul- ci ju - bi - lo_____ Now sing with hearts a- glow!_____
2. O Je - su, par- vu - le,_____ For thee I long al- way;_____

Our de - light and plea - sure Lies *in prae- se- pi - o,*_____ Like
Com- fort my heart's blind - ness, *O pu- er op- ti- me,*_____ With

sun - shine is our trea - sure *Ma- tris in gre- mi - o.*_____
all thy lov- ing- kind - ness, *O prin- ceps glo- ri- ae.*_____

*Al - pha es et O!*_____ *Al - pha es et O!*
*Tra - he me post te!*_____ *Tra - he me post te!*

The small notes in the last two bars are added to
preserve the usual version of the tune, and may be used if preferred.

3 *O Patris caritas!*
  O Nati lenitas!
    Deeply were we stainèd
  Per nostra crimina;
    But thou for us hast gainèd
  Coelorum gaudia.
  O that we were there!

4 *Ubi sunt gaudia*
  In any place but there?
    There are angels singing
  Nova cantica,
    And there the bells are ringing
  In Regis curia.
  O that we were there!

CHRISTMAS DAY

CHRISTMAS

Christmas has come, let's eat and drink—
This is no time to sit and think;
Farewell to study, books and pen,
And welcome to all kinds of men.
Let all men now get rid of care,
And what one has let others share;
Then 'tis the same, no matter which
Of us is poor, or which is rich.
Let each man have enough this day,
Since those that can are glad to pay;
There's nothing now too rich or good
For poor men, not the King's own food.
Now like a singing bird my feet
Touch earth, and I must drink and eat.
Welcome to all men: I'll not care
What any of my fellows wear;
We'll not let cloth divide our souls,
They'll swim stark naked in the bowls.
Welcome, poor beggar: I'll not see
That hand of yours dislodge a flea,
While you sit at my side and beg,
Or right foot scratching your left leg.
Farewell restraint: we will not now
Measure the ale our brains allow,
But drink as much as we can hold.
We'll count no change when we spend gold;
This is no time to save, but spend
To give for nothing, not to lend.
Let foes make friends: let them forget
The mischief-making dead that fret
The living with complaint like this—
"He wronged us once, hate him and his."
Christmas has come; let every man
Eat, drink, be merry all he can.
Ale's my best mark, but if port wine
Or whisky's yours—let it be mine;
No matter what lies in the bowls,
We'll make it rich with our own souls.
Farewell to study, books and pen,
And welcome to all kinds of men.

W. H. Davies

From Charles Dickens' "The Pickwick Papers"

CHRISTMAS AT DINGLEY DELL

FROM the centre of the ceiling . . . old Wardle had just suspended, with his own hands, a huge branch of mistletoe, and this same branch of mistletoe instantaneously gave rise to a scene of general and delightful scrambling and confusion; in the midst of which, Mr Pickwick with a gallantry that would have done honour to a descendant of Lady Tollimglower herself, took the old lady by the hand, led her beneath the mystic branch, and saluted her in all courtesy and decorum. The old lady submitted to this piece of practical politeness with all the dignity which befitted so important and serious a solemnity, but the younger ladies not being so thoroughly imbued with a superstitious veneration for the custom: or imagining that the value of a salute is very much enhanced if it cost a little trouble to obtain it: screamed and struggled, and ran into corners, and threatened and remonstrated, and did everything but leave the room, until some of the less adventurous gentlemen were on the point of desisting, when they all at once found it useless to resist any longer, and submitted to be kissed with a good grace. Mr Winkle kissed the young lady with the black eyes, and Mr Snodgrass kissed Emily, and Mr Weller, not being particular about the form of being under the mistletoe, kissed Emma and the other female servants, just as he caught them. As to the poor relations, they kissed everybody, not even excepting the plainer portions of the young-lady visitors, who, in their excessive confusion, ran right under the mistletoe, as soon as it was hung up, without knowing it! Wardle stood with his back to the fire, surveying the whole scene, with the utmost satisfaction; and the fat boy took the opportunity of appropriating to his own use, and summarily devouring, a particularly fine mince-pie, that had been carefully put by for somebody else.

Now, the screaming had subsided, and faces were in a glow, and curls in a tangle, and Mr Pickwick, after kissing the old lady as before mentioned, was standing under the mistletoe, looking with a very pleased countenance on all that was passing around him, when the young lady with the black eyes, after a little whispering with the other young ladies, made a sudden dart forward, and, putting her arm round Mr Pickwick's neck, saluted him affectionately on the left cheek; and before Mr Pickwick distinctly knew what was the matter, he was surrounded by the whole body, and kissed by every one of them.

It was a pleasant thing to see Mr Pickwick in the centre of the group, now
pulled this way, and then that, and first kissed on the chin, and then on the nose,
and then on the spectacles: and to hear the peals of laughter which were raised
on every side; but it was a still more pleasant thing to see Mr Pickwick, blinded
shortly afterwards with a silk handkerchief, falling up against the wall, and
scrambling into corners, and going through all the mysteries of blind-man's buff,
with the utmost relish for the game, until at last he caught one of the poor relations
and then had to evade the blind-man himself, which he did with a nimbleness and
agility that elicited the admiration and applause of all beholders. The poor relations
caught the people who they thought would like it, and, when the game flagged,
got caught themselves. When they were all tired of blind-man's buff, there was a
great game at snap-dragon, and when fingers enough were burned with that, and

all the raisins were gone, they sat down by the huge fire of blazing logs to a sub-
stantial supper, and a mighty bowl of wassail, something smaller than an ordinary
wash-house copper, in which the hot apples were hissing and bubbling with a rich
look, and a jolly sound, that were perfectly irresistible.

"This," said Mr Pickwick, looking round him, "this is, indeed, comfort."

"Our invariable custom," replied Mr Wardle. "Everybody sits down with us
on Christmas Eve, as you see them now—servants and all; and here we wait,
until the clock strikes twelve, to usher Christmas in, and beguile the time with
forfeits and old stories. Trundle, my boy, rake up the fire."

Up flew the bright sparks in myriads as the logs were stirred. The deep red blaze
sent forth a rich glow, that penetrated into the furthest corner of the room, and
cast its cheerful tint on every face.

THE TROUBLE WITH PRESENTS

What do you want
   On Christmas morning
What do you look forward to
   On Christmas day?
I don't care what *I* find
   In my Christmas stocking
So long as it's a game
   That only *one* can play.

I'm tired of always getting
   On Christmas morning
To keep me amused through
   The whole of Christmas day
Boxes of cards
   Or Snakes and Ladders
And games that only *two*
   Or *more* can play.

No wonder King John
   Was always furious
No wonder he ranted
   On Christmas day,
And craved for and *craved* for
   A red rubber ball
For a ball is a present
   With which *one* can play.

Though I'm not so sure
    Now I think about it!
Have you ever tried to play
    With a ball indoors?
It's sure to smash all
    The ornaments and vases
Or get stuck out of reach
    Behind a chest of drawers.

And you can't go outside
    Because it's snowing like fury
Or the rain's tipping down
    In buckets from the sky;
And the temperature's dropped
    With a thud below zero
And if you step out in that
    You're sure to freeze and die!

There's a box of candy
    That will 'spoil my dinner'
Or worse is sure to make me
    Feel 'frightfully sick'
And there's no point in learning
    My new conjuring game
If there's nobody available
    To enjoy the trick.

What's the point of having
    On Christmas morning
A present that requires
    A horde of other folks;
Even a fun book's
    Not so very funny
If you can't discover anyone
    To laugh at the jokes.

I'm fed up with Shepherds
    On Christmas morning
They had each other
    To share in their fun ;
Even those globe trotting
    Kings make me furious
As *they'd* have been furious
    If they'd been just *one* !

What about a book
    On Christmas morning?
Who wants to settle
    In a corner alone
Reading Milton's *Ode*
    On Christ's Nativity !
That's enough to make a
    Christmas Angel moan !

Every time I wake up
    On Christmas morning
I know what's going to happen
    As the day wears on ;
Every time I ask my parents
    To play with me
They're going to say 'O
    Not now. Later, son !'

For Mother's all snarled up
    Cooking the turkey:
'Now I'm sure you wouldn't want
    To eat it all raw!
Can't you go and play
    By yourself for a moment!
Where are all those super
    New toys I saw?'

But I can't blow my whistle
    Or thump my tin drum,
Or Dad whose feeling 'fragile'
    Will blow a fuse!
Though why they gave them to me
    In the first place, beats me,
Out of all the other
    Presents they could choose!

Well, the train looks wizard
    But I daren't lay down the tracks,
For they take up so much space
    That they'd get in the way.
Oh why can't some genius
    Invent for Christmas morning
A really super game
    That only *one* can play.

                    John Smith

HOODOO McFIGGIN'S CHRISTMAS

THIS Santa Claus business is played out. It's a sneaking underhand method, and the sooner it's exposed the better.

For a parent to get up under cover of the darkness of the night and palm off a ten-cent necktie on a boy who had been expecting a ten-dollar watch, and then say that an angel sent it to him, is low, undeniably low.

I had a good opportunity of observing how the thing worked this Christmas, in the case of young Hoodoo McFiggin, the son and heir of the McFiggins, at whose house I board.

Hoodoo McFiggin is a good boy—a religious boy. He had been given to understand that Santa Claus would bring nothing to his father and mother because grown-up people don't get presents from the angels. So he saved up all his pocket-money and bought a box of cigars for his father and a seventy-five-cent diamond brooch for his mother. His own fortunes he left in the hands of the angels. But he prayed. He prayed every night for weeks that Santa Claus would bring him a pair of skates and a puppy-dog and an air-gun and a bicycle and a Noah's ark and a sleigh and a drum—altogether about a hundred and fifty dollars' worth of stuff.

I went into Hoodoo's room quite early Christmas morning. I had an idea that the scene would be interesting. I woke him up and he sat up in bed, his eyes glistening with radiant expectation, and began hauling things out of his stocking.

The first parcel was bulky; it was done up quite loosely and had an odd look generally.

"Ha! ha!" Hoodoo cried gleefully, as he began undoing it. "I'll bet it's the puppy-dog, all wrapped up in paper!"

And was it the puppy-dog? No, by no means. It was a pair of nice, strong, number-four boots, laces and all, labelled, "Hoodoo, from Santa Claus," and underneath Santa Claus had written "95c net."

The boy's jaw fell with delight. "It's boots," he said, and plunged in his hand again.

He began hauling away at another parcel with renewed hope on his face.

This time the thing seemed like a little round box. Hoodoo tore the paper off it with a feverish hand. He shook it; something rattled inside.

"It's a watch and chain! It's a watch and chain!" he shouted. Then he pulled the lid off.

And was it a watch and chain? No. It was a box of nice, brand-new celluloid collars, a dozen of them all alike and all his own size.

The boy was so pleased that you could see his face crack up with pleasure.

He waited a few minutes until his intense joy subsided. Then he tried again.

This time the packet was long and hard. It resisted the touch and had a sort of funnel shape.

"It's a toy pistol," said the boy, trembling with excitement, "Gee! I hope there are lots of caps with it! I'll fire some off now and wake up father."

No, my poor child, you will not wake your father with that. It is a useful thing, but it needs not caps and it fires no bullets and you cannot wake a sleeping man with a tooth-brush. Yes, it was a tooth-brush—a regular beauty, pure bone all through, and ticketed with a little paper, "Hoodoo, from Santa Claus."

Again the expression of intense joy passed over the boy's face, and the tears of gratitude started from his eyes. He wiped them away with his tooth-brush and passed on.

The next parcel was much larger and evidently contained something soft and bulky. It had been too long to go in the stocking and was tied outside.

"I wonder what this is," Hoodoo mused, half afraid to open it. Then his heart gave a great leap, and he forgot all his other presents in the anticipation of this one. "It's a drum!" he gasped, "It's the drum, all wrapped up!"

Drum nothing! It was pants—a pair of the nicest little short pants—with dear little stripes of colour running across both ways, and here again Santa Claus had written "Hoodoo, from Santa Claus, one forty net."

But there was something wrapped up in it. Oh, yes! There was a pair of braces wrapped up in it, braces with a little steel sliding thing so that you could slide your pants up to your neck if you wanted to.

The boy gave a dry sob of satisfaction. Then he took out his last present. "It's a book," he said, as he unwrapped it. "I wonder if it is fairy stories or adventures! I'll read it all morning."

No, Hoodoo, it was not precisely adventures. It was a small family Bible. Hoodoo had now seen all his presents, and he arose and dressed. But he still had the fun of playing with his toys. That is always the chief delight of Christmas morning.

First he played with his tooth-brush. He got a whole lot of water and brushed all his teeth with it. This was huge.

Then he played with his collars. He had no end of fun with them, taking them all out one by one and swearing at them, and then putting them back and swearing at the whole lot together.

The next toy was his pants. He had immense fun there, putting them on and taking them off again, and then trying to guess which side was which by merely looking at them.

After that he took his book and read some adventures called "Genesis" till breakfast-time.

Then he went downstairs, and kissed his father and mother. His father was smoking a cigar, and his mother had her new brooch on. Hoodoo's face was thoughtful, and a light seemed to have broken in upon his mind. Indeed, I do think it altogether likely that next Christmas he will hang on to his own money and take chances on what the angels bring.

THE GIFT

As the wise men of old brought gifts
   guided by a star
      to the humble birthplace
of the god of love,
   the devils
      as an old print shows
retreated in confusion.

   What could a baby know
      of gold ornaments
or frankincense and myrrh,
   of priestly robes
      and devout genuflections?
But the imagination
   knows all stories
      before they are told
and knows the truth of this one
   past all defection.

The rich gifts
   so unsuitable for a child
      though devoutly proffered,
stood for all that love can bring.
   The men were old
      how could they know
of a mother's needs
   or a child's
    appetite?

But as they kneeled
    the child was fed.
        They saw it
and
    gave praise !

A miracle
    had taken place,
        hard gold to love,
a mother's milk !
    Before
        their wondering eyes.

The ass brayed
    the cattle lowed.
        It was their nature.

All men by their nature give praise.
    It is all
        they can do.

The very devils
    by their flight give praise.
        What is death,
beside this ?

    Nothing. The wise men
        came with gifts
and bowed down
    to worship
        this perfection.

                    William Carlos Williams

From "Menus for Every Day of the Year" (about 1900)
CHRISTMAS DAY

Breakfast
Eggs in Tomatoes
Tongue Toast
Fried Whiting

Luncheon
Stuffed Leaks
Roast Turkey
Plum Pudding

Dinner
Clear Soup
Macedoine of Sweetbreads
Braised Fillet of Beef
Boned Quail
Mince Pies
Chocolate Alexandra
Poire Melba

Servants' Dinner
Brown Soup
Roast Turkey
Plum Pudding

From Hesketh Pearson's "Bernard Shaw: His Life and Personality"

SHAW AND CHRISTMAS

EXCEPT when his health was shattered and he was bedridden he [Shaw] could scarcely remain inert for twenty consecutive minutes. Yet he made desperate attempts to take things easy. At Christmas, 1889, for example, he nearly drove himself mad in a vain effort to achieve repose. The carol-singers started him off: "The only music I have heard this week is Waits. To sit up working until two or three in the morning, and then, just as I am losing myself in my first sleep, to hear *Venite adoremus*, more generally known as Ow, cam let Haz adore Im, welling forth from a cornet (English pitch), a saxhorn (Society of Arts pitch, or thereabouts), and a trombone (French pitch), is the sort of thing that breaks my peace and destroys my good will towards men. Coming on top of a very arduous month, it reduced me last Saturday to a condition of such complete addledness, that it became evident that my overwrought brain would work itself soft in another fortnight unless an interval of complete mental vacuity could be induced. . . . Somebody suggested Broadstairs."

So to Broadstairs he went. "I am staying in Nuckell's Place; and they tell me that Miss Nuckell was the original of Betsey Trotwood in *David Copperfield*, and that the strip of green outside is that from which she used to chase the donkeys. A house down to the left is called Bleak House; and I can only say that if it is any bleaker than my bedroom, it must be a nonpareil freezer . . . Impelled to restless activity by the abominable ozone, I rushed off to the left; sped along the cliffs; passed a lighthouse, which looked as if it had been turned into a pillar of salt by the sea air; fell presently among stony ground; passed on into muddy ground; and finally reached Margate, a most dismal hole, where the iodine and ozone were flavoured with lodgings.

"I made at once for the railway station, and demanded the next train. 'Where to?' said the official. 'Anywhere,' I replied, 'provided it be far inland.' 'Train to Ramsgit at two-fifteen,' he said: 'nothing else till six.' I could not conceive Ramsgit as being so depressing even on Christmas Day, as Margit; so I got into that train; and, lo, the second station we came to was Broadstairs. This was the finger of Fate; for the ozone had made me so ragingly hungry that I burst from the train and ran all the way to Nuckell's Place, where, to my unspeakable horror and loathing, they triumphantly brought me up turkey with sausages. 'Surely, sir,' they said, as if remonstrating with me for some exhibition of depravity, '*surely* you eat meat on *Christmas* day.' 'I tell you,' I screamed, 'that I never eat meat.' 'Not even a little gravy, sir? I think it would do you good.' I put a fearful constraint on myself, and politely refused. Yet they came up again, as fresh as paint, with a discoloured mass of suet scorched in flaming brandy; and when I conveyed to them, as considerately as I could, that I thought the distinction between suet and meat, burnt brandy and spirits too fine to be worth insisting on, they evidently regarded me as hardly reasonable. There can be no doubt that the people here are mentally enfeebled. The keen air causes such rapid waste of tissue that they dare not add to it by thinking. They are always recuperating – that is to say eating – mostly cows." . . .

Another Christmas he spent "in an old-English manor-house,[1] where we all agreed to try and forget the festive season". But they were not wholly successful because a troupe of local mummers came in one evening and gave an operatic entertainment that was the reverse of entertaining: "We of the audience had to assume the character of good old English gentlemen and ladies keeping up a seasonable custom; and it would be difficult to say whether we or the performers were the more out of countenance. I have seldom been so disconcerted, and my host, though he kept it up amazingly, confessed to sharing my feelings; whilst the eagerness of the artists to escape from our presence when their performance was concluded and suitably acknowledged, testified to the total failure of our efforts to make them feel at home. We were perfectly friendly at heart, and would have been delighted to sit round the fire with them and talk; but the conventions of the season forbad it. Since we had to be mock-baronial, they had to be mock-servile; and so we made an uneasy company of Christmas humbugs, and had nothing to cheer us except the consciousness of heartily forgiving one another and being forgiven."

[1] William Morris's, Kelmscott Manor

SWEDISH ANGEL

The Swedish angel is nine inches high and shaped all of blonde straw.
All of blonde straw is her little body and her great seven-inch wings.
Her small head is of painted wood and she stands on a slim wood base.
Shining and shining in the Christmas candles, shines her golden halo.

Even all round her is a kind of shining, circle on circle, because
She has—it seems—lighted upon a round lake of clear glass
Surrounded by ground-pine and red berries which gleam also
In the candlelight that moves on her stilled blonde wings.

In this immaculate doll of heaven has been conceived, as though
No hands had shaped her, an uninvented innocence bequeathing grace
Ring upon ring in haloes all around her, and not remote nor kind
But only there, dispensing of all the brought light a total larger light.

Even now her wings have assumed such shields of glory and the pool beneath
Wheels with such wreaths of shining, the room is gathered and filled
By her tall and burning stillness and, an actual angel, her suspension wars
For a whole minute against all the dark, as if I were a child.

Winfield Townley Scott

LUBBERLU

"Green were her eyes—yellow were her eyes—
Her eyes were like withered sedge !"
—"This is holy Mass and the hour flies
And there is red in the church-yard hedge.

"Raise me aloft my taper's flame,
Light me my candles three,
For I must call on the Baby's name
Who is born to young Mary !"—

"O father, I see a blood-red streak
In the reeds where first I caught her—
And I hear a cry makes my heart weak—
And turns my bones to water.

"The marsh-bittern and lone curlew,
That cry comes not from them—"
—"Bring me bread and wine, my Lubberlu,
And hold my vestments' hem !

"The candles burn – The oxen kneel.
Boy, bring me my holy book—
Born is the King of Israel !"
—"Oh father, my father, look !

"She is pressing her face 'gainst the window-pane,
Where the saints stare in a row,
And her lips are red with the morning's stain
And her cheeks are white like snow !"

—"'Tis Christmas morn and the mass unsung
For the Baby of young Mary !"
But the idiot-boy from his side had sprung.
At the window prone was he.

And the oxen knelt in their frozen shed
And the sheep in their hurdled pen;
But Lubberlu lay stark and dead,
He never will come again.

They sign his breast and they sign his brow
With the cross to which they pray—
But two lost souls are flying now
Over the reeds and over the snow,
Over the hills and away.

John Cowper Powys

From Charles Dickens' "Christmas Stories"

A CHRISTMAS TREE

I have been looking on, this evening, at a merry company of children assembled round that pretty German toy, a Christmas Tree. The tree was planted in the middle of a great round table, and towered high above their heads. It was brilliantly lighted by a multitude of little tapers; and everywhere sparkled and glittered with bright objects. There were rosy-cheeked dolls, hiding behind the green leaves; and there were real watches (with movable hands, at least, and an endless capacity of being wound up) dangling from innumerable twigs; there were French-polished tables, chairs, bedsteads, wardrobes, eight-day clocks, and various other articles of domestic furniture (wonderfully made, in tin, at Wolverhampton), perched among the boughs, as if in preparation for some fairy housekeeping; there were jolly broadfaced men, much more agreeable in appearance than many real men—and no wonder, for their heads took off, and showed them to be full of sugar-plums; there were fiddles and drums; there were tambourines, books, work-boxes, paint-boxes, sweetmeat-boxes, peep-show boxes, and all kinds of boxes; there were trinkets for the elder girls, far brighter than any grown-up gold and jewels . . . there were guns, swords and banners, pen-wipers, smelling-bottles, real fruit . . . imitation apples, pears and walnuts, crammed with surprises; . . . in short, as a pretty child delightedly whispered to another pretty child, "There was everything, and more."

Being now at home again, and alone, the only person in the house awake, my thoughts are drawn back, by a fascination which I do not care to resist, to my own childhood. I begin to consider, what do we all remember best upon the branches of the Christmas Tree of our own young Christmas days, by which we climbed to real life?

Straight, in the middle of the room, cramped in the freedom of its growth by no encircling walls or soon-reached ceiling, a shadowy tree arises; and, looking up into the dreamy brightness of its top—for I observe in this tree the singular property that it appears to grow downwards towards the earth—I look into my youngest Christmas recollection. . . .

I see a wonderful row of little lights rise smoothly out of the ground, before a vast green curtain. Now a bell rings—a magic bell, which still sounds in my ears unlike all other bells—and music plays, amidst a buzz of voices, and a fragrant smell of orange-peel. Anon, the magic bell commands the music to cease, and the great green curtain rolls itself up majestically, and The Play begins. . . . Out of this delight springs the toy-theatre—there it is, with its familiar proscenium, and ladies in feathers, in the boxes!—and all its attendant occupation with paste and glue, and gum, and water colours, in the getting-up of The Miller and his Men. . . .

Vast is the crop of such fruit, shining on our Christmas Tree; in blossom, almost at the very top; ripening all down the boughs!

Among the later toys and fancies hanging there—as idle often and less pure—be the images once associated with the sweet old Waits, the softened music in the night, ever unalterable! Encircled by the social thoughts of Christmas-time, still let the benignant figure of my childhood stand unchanged! In every cheerful image and suggestion that the season brings, may the bright star that rested above the poor roof, be the star of all the Christian world! A moment's pause, O vanishing tree, of which the lower branches are dark to me as yet, and let me look once more! I know there are blank spaces on thy branches, where eyes that I have loved have looked and smiled; from which they are departed. But far above, I see the raiser of the dead girl, and the Widow's Son; and God is good! If age be hiding for me in the unseen portion of thy downward growth, O may I, with a grey head, turn a child's heart to that figure yet, and a child's trustfulness and confidence!

Now, the tree is decorated with bright merriment, and song, and dance, and cheerfulness. And they are welcome. Innocent and welcome be they ever held, beneath the branches of the Christmas Tree, which cast no gloomy shadow!

THE CHRISTMAS TREE

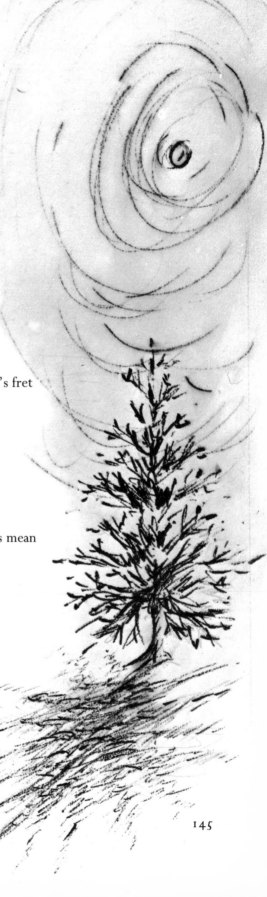

Put out the lights now !
Look at the Tree, the rough tree dazzled
In oriole plumes of flame,
Tinselled with twinkling frost fire, tasselled
With stars and moons—the same
That yesterday hid in the spinney and had no fame
Till we put out the lights now.

Hard are the nights now :
The fields at moonrise turn to agate,
Shadows are cold as jet ;
In dyke and furrow, in copse and faggot
The frost's tooth is set ;
And stars are the sparks whirled out by the North wind's fret
On the flinty nights now.

So feast your eyes now
On mimic star and moon-cold bauble :
Worlds may wither unseen,
But the Christmas Tree is a tree of fable,
A phoenix in evergreen,
And the world cannot change or chill what its mysteries mean
To your hearts and eyes now.

The vision dies now
Candle by candle : the tree that embraced it
Returns to its own kind,
To be earthed again and weather as best it
May the frost and the wind.
Children, it too had its hour—you will not mind
If it lives or dies now.

C. Day Lewis

145

From Mrs Glasse's "The Art of Cookery made Plain and Easy"

CHRISTMAS FARE

THE best way to roast a Turkey is to loosen the skin on the Breast of the Turkey, and fill it with Force-Meat, made thus: Take a Quarter of a Pound of Beef Sewet, as many Crumbs of Bread, a little Lemon peel, an Anchovy, some Nutmeg, Pepper, Parsley and a little Thyme. Chop and beat them all well together, mix them with the Yolk of an Egg, and stuff up the Breast; when you have no Sewet, Butter will do; or you may make some Force-Meat thus: Spread Bread and Butter thin, and grate some Nutmeg over it; when you have enough, roll it up, and stuff the Breast of the Turkey; then roast it of a fine Brown, but be sure to pin some white Paper on the Breast till it is near enough [done]. You must have a good gravy in the Dish, and Bread-Sauce, made thus: Take a good piece of Crumb, put it into a pint of Water, with a blade or two of Mace, two or three Cloves, and some Whole Pepper. Boil it up five or six times, then with a spoon take out the Spice you had before put in, and then you must pour off the Water (you may boil an Onion in it if you please) then beat up the Bread with a good piece of Butter and a little Salt.

Anthelme Brillat-Savarin

THE ORIGINS OF THE TURKEY

THE Turkey is surely one of the prettiest presents which the Old World has received from the New. I have been at some pains to investigate the subject, and here are my conclusions:

1. That the Turkey appeared in Europe towards the end of the seventeenth century.

2. That it was imported by the Jesuits, who bred it in large numbers, particularly on one of their farms in the neighbourhood of Bourges.

3. That from there it gradually spread over the whole of France; and hence it was that in many dialects the word for Turkey became and still is *jesuite*.

4. That America is the only place where the Turkey has been found wild and in a state of nature (there are none in Africa).

5. That in North America, where it is very common, they rear it either from eggs found in the forest and hatched in captivity, or from young birds caught wild; so reared, it is nearer to its natural state, and retains its primitive plumage.

From Michael Bond's "More About Paddington"
PADDINGTON'S CHRISTMAS

PADDINGTON found that Christmas took a long time to come. Each morning when he hurried downstairs he crossed the date off the calendar, but the more days he crossed off the farther away it seemed.

However, there was plenty to occupy his mind. For one thing, the postman started arriving later and later in the morning, and when he did finally reach the Browns' house there were so many letters to deliver he had a job to push them all through the letter-box. Often there were mysterious-looking parcels as well, which Mrs Bird promptly hid before Paddington had time to squeeze them.

A surprising number of the envelopes were addressed to Paddington himself, and he carefully made a list of all those who had sent him Christmas cards so that he could be sure of thanking them.

"You may be only a small bear," said Mrs Bird, as she helped him arrange the cards on the mantelpiece, "but you certainly leave your mark."

Paddington wasn't sure how to take this, especially as Mrs Bird had just polished the hall floor, but when he examined his paws they were quite clean.

Paddington had made his own Christmas cards. Some he had drawn himself, decorating the edges with holly and mistletoe; others had been made out of pictures cut from Mrs Brown's magazines. But each one had the words A MERRY CHRISTMAS AND A HAPPY NEW YEAR printed on the front, and they were signed PADINGTUN BROWN on the inside—together with his special paw mark to show that they were genuine.

Paddington wasn't sure about the spelling of A MERRY CHRISTMAS. It didn't look at all right. But Mrs Bird checked all the words in a dictionary for him to make certain.

"I don't suppose many people get Christmas cards from a bear," she explained. "They'll probably want to keep them, so you ought to make sure they are right."

One evening Mr Brown arrived home with a huge Christmas tree tied to the roof of his car. It was placed in a position of honour by the dining-room window and both Paddington and Mr Brown spent a long time decorating it with coloured lights and silver tinsel.

Apart from the Christmas tree, there were paper chains and holly to be put up, and large coloured bells made of crinkly paper. Paddington enjoyed doing the paper chains. He managed to persuade Mr Brown that bears were very good at putting up decorations and together they did most of the house, with Paddington standing on Mr Brown's shoulders while Mr Brown handed up the drawing pins. It came to an unhappy end one evening when Paddington accidentally put his paw on a drawing pin which he'd left on top of Mr Brown's head. When Mrs Bird rushed into the dining-room to see what all the fuss was about, and to inquire why all the lights had suddenly gone out, she found Paddington hanging by his paws from the chandelier and Mr Brown dancing around the room rubbing his head.

But by then the decorations were almost finished and the house had taken on quite a festive air. The sideboard was groaning under the weight of nuts and oranges, dates and figs, none of which Paddington was allowed to touch, and Mr Brown had stopped smoking his pipe and was filling the air instead with the smell of cigars.

The excitement in the Brown's house mounted, until it reached fever pitch a few days before Christmas, when Jonathan and Judy arrived home for the holidays.

But if the days leading up to Christmas were busy and exciting, they were nothing compared with Christmas day itself.

The Browns were up early on Christmas morning—much earlier than they had intended. It all started when Paddington woke to find a large pillow-case at the bottom of his bed. His eyes nearly popped out with astonishment when he switched his torch on, for it was bulging with parcels, and it certainly hadn't been there when he'd gone to bed on Christmas Eve.

Paddington's eyes grew larger and larger as he unwrapped the brightly coloured paper round each present. A few days before, on Mrs Bird's instructions, he had made a list of all the things he hoped to have given him and had hidden it up one of the chimneys. It was a strange thing, but everything on that list seemed to be in the pillow-case.

There was a large chemistry set from Mr Brown, full of jars and bottles and test tubes, which looked very interesting. And there was a miniature xylophone from Mrs Brown, which pleased him no end. Paddington was fond of music— especially the loud sort, which was good for conducting—and he had always wanted something he could actually play.

Mrs Bird's parcel was even more exciting, for it contained a checked cap which he'd specially asked for and had underlined on his list. Paddington stood on the end of his bed, admiring the effect in the mirror for quite a while.

Jonathan and Judy had each given him a travel book. Paddington was very interested in geography, being a much-travelled bear, and he was pleased to see there were plenty of maps and coloured pictures inside.

The noise from Paddington's room was soon sufficient to waken both Jonathan and Judy, and in no time at all the whole house was in an uproar, with wrapping paper and bits of string everywhere.

''I'm as patriotic as the next man,'' grumbled Mr Brown. ''But I draw the line when bears start playing the National Anthem at six o'clock in the morning— especially on a xylophone.'

As always, it was left to Mrs Bird to restore order. ''No more presents until after lunch,'' she said, firmly. She had just tripped over Paddington on the upstairs landing, where he was investigating his new chemical outfit, and something nasty had gone in one of her slippers.

149

"It's all right, Mrs Bird," said Paddington, consulting his instruction book, "it's only some iron filings. I don't think they're dangerous."

"Dangerous or not," said Mrs Bird, "I've a big dinner to cook—not to mention your birthday cake to finish decorating."

Being a bear, Paddington had two birthdays each year—one in the summer and one at Christmas—and the Browns were holding a party in his honour to which Mr Gruber had been invited.

After they'd had breakfast and been to church, the morning passed quickly and Paddington spent most of his time trying to decide what to do next. With so many things from which to choose it was most difficult. He read some chapters from his books and made several interesting smells and a small explosion with his chemical outfit.

Mr Brown was already in trouble for having given it to him, especially when Paddington found a chapter in the instruction book headed "Indoor Fireworks". He made himself a "never ending" snake which wouldn't stop growing and frightened Mrs Bird to death when she met it coming down the stairs.

"If we don't watch out," she confided to Mrs Brown, "we shan't last over Christmas. We shall either be blown to smithereens or poisoned. He was testing my gravy with some litmus paper just now."

Mrs Brown sighed. "It's a good job Christmas only comes once a year," she said, as she helped Mrs Bird with the potatoes.

"It isn't over yet," warned Mrs Bird.

Fortunately, Mr Gruber arrived at that moment and some measure of order was established before they all sat down to dinner.

Paddington's eyes glistened as he surveyed the table. He didn't agree with Mr Brown when he said it all looked too good to eat. All the same, even Paddington got noticeably slower towards the end when Mrs Bird brought in the Christmas pudding.

"Well," said Mr Gruber, a few minutes later, as he sat back and surveyed his empty plate, "I must say that's the best Christmas dinner I've had for many a day. Thank you very much indeed!"

"Hear! Hear!" agreed Mr Brown. "What do you say, Paddington?"

"It was very nice," said Paddington, licking some cream from his whiskers. "Except I had a bone in my Christmas pudding."

"You *what?*" exclaimed Mrs Brown. "Don't be silly—there are no bones in Christmas pudding."

"I had one," said Paddington, firmly. "It was all hard—and it stuck in my throat."

150

"Good gracious!" exclaimed Mrs Bird. "The sixpence! I always put a piece of silver in the Christmas pudding."

"What!" said Paddington, nearly falling off his chair. "A sixpence? I've never heard of a sixpence pudding before."

"Quick," shouted Mr Brown, rising to the emergency. "Turn him upside down."

Before Paddington could reply, he found himself hanging head downwards while Mr Brown and Mr Gruber took it in turns to shake him. The rest of the family stood round watching the floor.

"It's no good," said Mr Brown, after a while. "It must have gone too far." He helped Mr Gruber lift Paddington into an armchair, where he lay gasping for breath.

"I've got a magnet upstairs," said Jonathan. "We could try lowering it down his throat on a piece of string."

"I don't think so, dear," said Mrs Brown, in a worried tone of voice. "He might swallow that and then we should be even worse off." She bent over the chair. "How do you feel, Paddington?"

"Sick," said Paddington, in an aggrieved tone of voice.

"Of course you do, dear," said Mrs Brown. "It's only to be expected. There's only one thing to do—we shall have to send for the doctor."

"Thank goodness I scrubbed it first," said Mrs Bird. "It might have been covered with germs."

"But I *didn't* swallow it," gasped Paddington. "I only nearly did. Then I put it on the side of my plate. I didn't know it was a sixpence because it was all covered with Christmas pudding."

Paddington felt very fed up. He'd just eaten one of the best dinners he could ever remember and now he'd been turned upside down and shaken without even being given time to explain.

Everyone exchanged glances and then crept quietly away, leaving Paddington to recover by himself. There didn't seem to be much they *could* say.

But after the dinner things had been cleared away, and by the time Mrs Bird had made some strong coffee, Paddington was almost himself again. He was sitting up in the chair helping himself to some dates when they trooped back into the room. It took a lot to make Paddington ill for very long.

When they had finished their coffee, and were sitting round the blazing fire feeling warm and comfortable, Mr Brown rubbed his hands. "Now, Paddington," he said, "it's not only Christmas, it's your birthday as well. What would you like to do?"

A mysterious expression came over Paddington's face.

"If you all go in the other room," he announced, "I've a special surprise for you."

"Oh dear, *must* we, Paddington?" said Mrs Brown. "There isn't a fire."

"I shan't be long," said Paddington, firmly. "But it's a special surprise and it has to be prepared." He held the door open and the Browns, Mrs Bird, and Mr Gruber filed obediently into the other room.

"Now close your eyes," said Paddington, when they were settled, "and I'll let you know when I'm ready."

Mrs Brown shivered. "I hope you won't be too long," she called. But the only reply was the sound of the door clicking shut.

They waited for several minutes without speaking, and then Mr Gruber cleared his throat. "Do you think young Mr Brown's forgotten about us?" he asked.

"I don't know," said Mrs Brown. "But I'm not waiting much longer."

"Henry!" she exclaimed, as she opened her eyes. "Have you gone to sleep?"

"Er, wassat?" snorted Mr. Brown. He had eaten such a large dinner he was finding it difficult to keep awake. "What's happening? Have I missed anything?"

"Nothing's happening," said Mrs Brown. "Henry, you'd better go and see what Paddington's up to."

Several more minutes went by before Mr Brown returned to announce that he couldn't find Paddington anywhere.

"Well, he must be *somewhere*," said Mrs Brown. "Bears don't disappear into thin air."

"Crikey!" exclaimed Jonathan, as a thought suddenly struck him. "You don't think he's playing at Father Christmas, do you? He was asking all about it the other day when he put his list up the chimney. I bet that's why he wanted us to come in here—because this chimney connects with the one upstairs—and there isn't a fire."

"Father Christmas?" said Mr Brown. "I'll give him Father Christmas!" He stuck his head up the chimney and called Paddington's name several times. "I can't see anything," he said, striking a match. As if in answer a large lump of soot descended and burst on top of his head.

"Now look what you've done, Henry," said Mrs Brown. "Shouting so—you've disturbed the soot. All over your clean shirt!"

"If it *is* young Mr Brown, perhaps he's stuck somewhere," suggested Mr Gruber. "He did have rather a large dinner. I remember wondering at the time where he put it all."

Mr Gruber's suggestion had an immediate effect on the party and everyone began to look serious.

"Why, he might suffocate with the fumes," exclaimed Mrs Bird, as she hurried outside to the broom cupboard.

When she returned, armed with a mop, everyone took it in turns to poke it up the chimney but even though they strained their ears they couldn't hear a sound.

It was while the excitement was at its height that Paddington came into the room.

He looked most surprised when he saw Mr Brown with his head up the chimney.

"You can come into the dining-room now," he announced, looking round the room. "I've finished wrapping my presents and they're all on the Christmas tree."

"You don't mean to say," spluttered Mr Brown, as he sat in the fireplace rubbing his face with a handkerchief, "you've been in the other room all the time?"

"Yes," said Paddington, innocently. "I hope I didn't keep you waiting too long."

Mrs Brown looked at her husband. "I thought you said you'd looked everywhere," she exclaimed.

"Well—we'd just come from the dining-room," said Mr Brown, looking very sheepish. "I didn't think he'd be *there*."

"It only goes to show," said Mrs Bird hastily, as she caught sight of the expression on Mr Brown's face, "how easy it is to give a bear a bad name."

Paddington looked most interested when they explained to him what all the fuss was about.

"I never thought of coming down the chimney," he said, staring at the fireplace.

"Well, you're not thinking about it now either," replied Mr Brown, sternly.

But even Mr Brown's expression changed as he followed Paddington into the dining-room and saw the presents that had been prepared for them.

In addition to the presents that had already been placed on the tree, there were now six newly wrapped ones tied to the lower branches. If the Browns recognized the wrapping paper they had used for Paddington's presents earlier in the day, they were much too polite to say anything.

"I'm afraid I had to use old paper," said Paddington apologetically, as he waved a paw at the tree. "I hadn't any money left. That's why you had to go in the other room while I wrapped them."

"Really, Paddington," said Mrs Brown. "I'm very cross with you—spending all your money on presents for us."

"I'm afraid they're rather ordinary," said Paddington, as he settled back in a chair to watch the others. "But I hope you like them. They're all labelled so that you know which is which."

"Ordinary?" exclaimed Mr Brown, as he opened his parcel. "I don't call a pipe rack ordinary. And there's an ounce of my favourite tobacco tied to the back as well!"

"Gosh! A new stamp album!" cried Jonathan. "Whizzo! And it's got some stamps inside already."

"They're Peruvian ones from Aunt Lucy's postcards," said Paddington. "I've been saving them for you."

"And I've got a box of paints," exclaimed Judy. "Thank you very much, Paddington. It's just what I wanted."

"We all seem to be lucky," said Mrs Brown, as she unwrapped a parcel containing a bottle of her favourite lavender water. "How *did* you guess? I finished my last bottle only a week ago."

"I'm sorry about your parcel, Mrs Bird," said Paddington, looking across the room. "I had a bit of a job with the knots."

"It must be something special," said Mr Brown. "It seems all string and no parcel."

"That's because it's really clothes line," explained Paddington, "not string. I rescued it when I got stuck in the revolving door at Crumbold and Ferns."

"That makes two presents in one," said Mrs Bird, as she freed the last of the knots and began unwinding yards and yards of paper. "How exciting. I can't think what it can be."

"Why," she exclaimed. "I do believe it's a brooch! And it's shaped like a bear—how lovely!" Mrs Bird looked most touched as she handed the present round for everyone to see. "I shall keep it in a safe place," she added, "and only wear it on special occasions—when I want to impress people."

"I don't know what mine is," said Mr Gruber, as they all turned to him. He squeezed the parcel. "It's such a funny shape."

"It's a drinking mug!" he exclaimed, his face lighting up with pleasure. "And it even has my name painted on the side!"

"It's for your elevenses, Mr Gruber," said Paddington. "I noticed your old one was getting rather chipped."

"I'm sure it will make my cocoa taste better than it ever has before," said Mr Gruber.

He stood up and cleared his throat. "I think I would like to offer a vote of thanks to young Mr Brown," he said, "for all his nice presents. I'm sure he must have given them a great deal of thought."

"Hear! Hear!" echoed Mr Brown, as he filled his pipe.

Mr Gruber felt under his chair, "And while I think of it, Mr Brown, I have a small present for you."

Everyone stood round and watched while Paddington struggled with his parcel, eager to see what Mr Gruber had bought him. A gasp of surprise went up as he tore the paper to one side, for it was a beautifully bound leather scrapbook, with "Paddington Brown" printed in gold leaf on the cover.

Paddington didn't know what to say, but Mr Gruber waved his thanks to one side. "I know how you enjoy writing about your adventures, Mr Brown," he said. "And you have so many I'm sure your present scrapbook must be almost full."

"It is," said Paddington, earnestly. "And I'm sure I shall have lots more. Things happen to me, you know. But I shall only put by best ones in here!"

When he made his way up to bed later that evening, his mind was in such a whirl, and he was so full of good things, he could hardly climb the stairs—let alone think about anything. He wasn't quite sure which he had enjoyed most. The presents, the Christmas dinner, the games, or the tea—with the special marmalade-layer birthday cake Mrs Bird had made in his honour. Pausing on the corner half way up, he decided he had enjoyed giving his own presents best of all.

"Paddington! Whatever have you got there?" He jumped and hastily hid his paw behind his back as he heard Mrs Bird calling from the bottom of the stairs.

"It's only some sixpence pudding, Mrs Bird," he called, looking over the banisters guiltily. "I thought I might get hungry during the night and I didn't want to take any chances."

"Honestly!" Mrs Bird exclaimed, as she was joined by the others. "What *does* that bear look like? A paper hat about ten sizes too big on his head—Mr Gruber's scrapbook in one paw—and a plate of Christmas pudding in the other!"

"I don't care what he looks like," said Mrs Brown, "so long as he stays that way. The place wouldn't be the same without him."

But Paddington was too far away to hear what was being said. He was already sitting up in bed, busily writing in his scrapbook.

First of all, there was a very important notice to go on the front page. It said:

PADINGTUN BROWN,

32 WINDSOR GARDENS,

LUNDUN,

ENGLAND,

YUROPE,

THE WORLD

Then, on the next page he added, in large capital letters: MY ADDVENTURES. CHAPTER WUN.

Paddington sucked his pen thoughtfully for a moment and then carefully replaced the top on the bottle of ink before it had a chance to fall over on the sheets. He felt much too sleepy to write any more. But he didn't really mind. Tomorrow was another day – and he felt quite sure he *would* have some more adventures— even if he didn't know what they were going to be as yet.

Paddington lay back and pulled the blankets up round his whiskers. It was warm and comfortable and he sighed contentedly as he closed his eyes. It was nice being a bear. Especially a bear called Paddington.

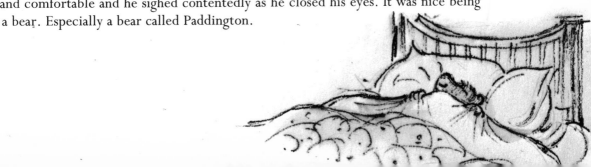

CHRISTMAS SCANDAL

"Christmas Tree,
  Green and white,
What do you say
  This festive night?"

"Nothing you'll like!   "Nobody cares
  What *can* I say?   About my plight—
The candles shine,   That any moment
  The children play;   I'll catch alight!

"Wax on my hair
  And round my throat,
Wax on my fine dark
  Winter coat;

"Wax on my hips
  And tingling flanks,
Hot wax trickling
  Down my shanks;

"Wax on my *toes*—   "Christmas Tree,
  But they're asleep,   Tall and spruce,
Clamped in the flower-pot,   Keep your pecker up!"
  Twisted deep!"   "What's the use?

"A clumsy push,
  A flame, a scare,
And they'll be dragging me
  By the hair!

"They always forget,
  The stupid vandals!
That's why I say,
  'Blow the candles!'"

William Kean Seymour

I SAW A STABLE

I saw a stable, low and very bare,
  A little child in a manger.
The oxen knew Him, had Him in their care,
  To men he was a stranger.
The safety of the world was lying there,
  And the world's danger.

Mary Elizabeth Coleridge

A CHRISTMAS CAROL

In the bleak mid-winter
   Frosty wind made moan,
Earth stood hard as iron,
   Water like a stone;
Snow had fallen, snow on snow,
   Snow on snow,
In the bleak mid-winter
    Long ago.

Our God, Heaven cannot hold Him,
   Nor earth sustain;
Heaven and earth shall flee away
   When He comes to reign:
In the bleak mid-winter
   A stable-place sufficed
The Lord God Almighty
   Jesus Christ.

Enough for Him, whom cherubim
   Worship night and day,
A breastful of milk,
   A mangerful of hay;
Enough for Him whom angels
   Fall down before,
The ox and ass and camel
   Which adore.

Angels and archangels
  May have gathered there;
Cherubim and seraphim
  Throng'd the air,
But only His Mother
  In her maiden bliss,
Worshipped the Beloved
    With a kiss.

What can I give Him,
  Poor as I am?
If I were a shepherd
  I would bring a lamb,
If I were a wise man
  I would do my part—
Yet what can I give Him?
    Give my heart.

Christina Rossetti

159

CAROL

A child was born in Judah
In the mid-hour of the night,
A Child was born in Judah
Under a new star's light;
With a plain gold ring about His brows
A Child was born to Judah's House.

There was no inn of Judah
That hung His crucial sign,
Nor cup nor board in Judah
Had held His Bread, His Wine:
No other byre in all the earth
Sheltered a Prince King at his birth.

—Long gone the gifts of sages,
The shepherd worshippers—
But truth outdares the ages
And love outlasts the years.
His angels' song has meaning still,
''Peace unto all men of goodwill.''

Carla Lanyon Lanyon

TO HIS SAVIOUR, A CHILD;
A PRESENT, BY A CHILD

Go pretty child, and bear this flower
Unto thy little Saviour;
And tell him, by that bud now blown,
He is the *Rose of Sharon* known:
When thou hast said so, stick it there
Upon his bib, or stomacher:
And tell him, (for good handsel[1] too)
That thou hast brought a whistle new,
Made of a clean straight oaten reed,
To charm his cries, (at time of need:)
Tell him, for coral, thou hast none;
But if thou hadst, he should have one;
But poor thou art, and known to be
Even as moneyless, as he,
Lastly if thou canst win a kiss
From those mellifluous lips of his,
Then never take a second one,
To spoil the first impression.

Robert Herrick

[1] present

JOSEPH

Who has not carolled Mary,
  And who her praise would dim?
But what of humble Joseph:
  Is there no song for him?

If Joseph had not driven
  Straight nails through honest wood;
If Joseph had not cherished
  His Mary as he should;

If Joseph had not proved him
  A sire both kind and wise:
Would he have drawn with favour
  The Child's all-probing eyes?

Would Christ have prayed "Our Father",
  Or cried that Name in death,
Unless he first had honoured
  Joseph of Nazareth?

Gilbert Thomas

From Leslie Daiken's "Children's Games throughout the Year"

ANNUAL MIRACLE

IN the full year's almanac of games and gladness, it is Christmastide when childhood's annual miracle takes place. The vision of Santa Claus breathlessly waited for: the thought of his coming, whether in his Continental role of benign Saint Nicholas, or as the red-robed, white-bearded jolly patriarch who rides on a reindeer-drawn sledge above the roofs, to the jingle of sleigh-bells nobody ever hears, excites and obsesses the child-consciousness. Each day is impatiently counted.

Then, somehow, all the magic and lore of time-old family tradition are summed up for the festival of peace and goodwill and good cheer. The cutting and hanging of holly sets the key for all the pageantry and party spirit that go with what has come to be known as "A White Christmas". The hanging of the mistletoe, its Druidic associations quite forgotten, means that Father Christmas is well set on his course from the Polar North and due to land very soon indeed.

The spangled tree, the candles and crackers and cake, the waits and the singing of carols, the dressing up for the school play, Nativity or Morality, the longed-for visits to pantomime, circus, toy bazaar gratified—all are overshadowed by the reality of the brimming sack.

Its bounty of toys, asked for, prayed for, and passionately expected, yet each one a surprise, crowns the season when, first thought on waking, the stocking's owner runs to the chimney-piece or the bed-rail to seek and find his heart's desire.

The custom of the Christmas-tree was brought to England from the Continent, when Queen Victoria introduced it into her household. After that it was popularized rapidly and has since come to be regarded as part of the British Christmas tradition.

LET'S HAVE MUSIC

Lett no man cum into this hall,
Grome, page, nor yet marshall,
But that sum sport he bryng withall;
 For now ys the tyme of Crystymas!

Yff that he say he can not sing
Some oder sport then let him bring,
That yt may please at thys festyng;
 For now ys the tyme of Crystymas!

Yff he say he can nowght do,
Then for my love aske hym no mo,
But to the stokkis then lett hym go;
 For now ys the tyme of Crystymas!

Richard Hill

A CAROL FOR THE CHILDREN

God rest you merry, Innocents,
Let nothing you dismay,
Let nothing wound an eager heart
Upon this Christmas day.

Yours be the genial holly wreaths,
The stockings and the tree;
An aged world to you bequeaths
Its own forgotten glee.

Soon, soon enough come crueller gifts,
The anger and the tears;
Between you now there sparsely drifts
A handful yet of years.

Oh, dimly, dimly glows the star
Through the electric throng;
The bidding in temple and bazaar
Drowns out the silver song.

The ancient altars smoke afresh,
The ancient idols stir;
Faint in the reek of burning flesh
Sink frankincense and myrrh.

Gaspar, Balthazar, Melchior!
Where are your offerings now?
What greetings to the Prince of War,
His darkly branded brow?

Two ultimate laws alone we know,
The ledger and the sword—
So far away, so long ago,
We lost the infant Lord.

Only the children clasp His hand;
His voice speaks low to them,
And still for them the shining band
Wings over Bethlehem.

God rest you merry, Innocents,
While innocence endures,
A sweeter Christmas than we to ours
May you bequeath to yours.

Ogden Nash

THE CHRISTMAS STORY IN THE GOSPELS

From the Gospel according to St Luke

THE SHEPHERDS

AND it came to pass in those days, that there went out a decree from Caesar Augustus, that all the world should be taxed. And all went to be taxed, everyone into his own city.

And Joseph also went up from Galilee, out of the city of Nazareth, into Judaea, unto the city of David, which is called Bethlehem; (because he was of the house and lineage of David:) to be taxed with Mary his espoused wife, being great with child.

And so it was, that, while they were there, the days were accomplished that she should be delivered. And she brought forth her firstborn son, and wrapped him in swaddling clothes, and laid him in a manger; because there was no room for them in the inn.

And there were in the same country shepherds abiding in the field, keeping watch over their flock by night. And, lo, the angel of the Lord came upon them, and the glory of the Lord shone round about them: and they were sore afraid.

And the angel said unto them, Fear not; for, behold, I bring you good tidings of great joy, which shall be to all people. For unto you is born this day in the city of David a Saviour, which is Christ the Lord. And this shall be a sign unto you; ye shall find the babe wrapped in swaddling clothes, lying in a manger.

And suddenly there was with the angel a multitude of the heavenly host praising God, and saying, Glory to God in the highest, and on earth peace, good will toward men.

And it came to pass, as the angels were gone away from them into heaven, the shepherds said one to another, Let us now go even unto Bethlehem, and see this thing which has come to pass, which the Lord hath made known unto us.

And they came with haste, and found Mary, and Joseph, and the babe lying in a manger. And when they had seen it, they made known abroad the saying which was told them concerning this child. And all they that heard it wondered at those things which were told them by the shepherds. But Mary kept all these things, and pondered them in her heart. And the shepherds returned, glorifying and praising God for all the things that they had heard and seen, as it was told unto them.

From the Gospel according to St Matthew

THE WISE MEN

Now when Jesus was born in Bethlehem of Judaea in the days of Herod the king, behold, there came wise men from the east to Jerusalem, saying, Where is he that is born King of the Jews? for we have seen his star in the east, and are come to worship him.

When Herod the king had heard these things, he was troubled, and all Jerusalem with him. And when he had gathered all the chief priests and scribes of the people together, he demanded of them where Christ should be born.

And they said unto him, In Bethlehem of Judaea; for thus it is written by the prophet:

'And thou, Bethlehem, in the land of Juda,
Art not the least among the princes of Juda:
For out of thee shall come a Governor,
That shall rule my people Israel.'

Then Herod, when he had privily called the wise men, inquired of them diligently what time the star appeared. And he sent them to Bethlehem, and said, Go and search diligently for the young child; and when ye have found him, bring me word again, that I may come and worship him also.

When they had heard the king, they departed; and, lo, the star, which they saw in the east, went before them, till it came and stood over where the young child was. When they saw the star, they rejoiced with exceeding great joy. And when they were come into the house, they saw the young child with Mary his mother, and fell down, and worshipped him: and when they had opened their treasures, they presented unto him gifts; gold, and frankincense, and myrrh.

MARY AND HER CHILD

A lovely lady sat and sange
  And to her son thus gan she say:
"My son, my lord, my dere darling,
  Why liggis[1] thou thus in hay?
    Myn own dere son,
    How art thou cum,
  Art thou not God verey?[2]
    But never the lesse
    I will not cease
  To sing 'by, by, lully, lulley.'"

Then spake the child that was so young
  And thus me thought he said:
"I am knowen as heaven king,
  In crib though I now be laid;
  Thou knowest it is no hay.
    Angellis bright
    To me shall light;
    And of that sight
    Ye may be light,
  And sing 'by, by, lully, lulley.'"

"Jesu, my son, heaven king,
  Why lyest thou thus in stall?
And why hast thou no rich bedding
  In sum rich kings hall?
    Me thinketh by right,
    The lord of might
    Should lie in rich array;
    But never the lesse
    I will not cease
  To sing 'by, by, lully, lulley.'"

[1] liest   [2] truly

"Mary mother, queen of bliss,
　Me thinketh it is no law
That I should go to the kingis
　And they not to me draw;
　　But you shall see
　　That kingis three
　To me will cum on the twelfth day;
　　For this beheste
　　Give me your breast,
And sing 'by, by, lully, lulley.'"

"Jesu, my son, I pray thee, say,
　As thou art to me dear:
How shall I serve thee to thy pay,
　And make thee right good cheer?
　　All thy will
　　I would fulfill,
　Thou knowest it well in fay;
　　But rock thee still
　　And dance thee there-till,
And sing 'by, by, lully lulley.'"

"Mary, mother, I pray thee,
　Take me up on loft,
And in thyn arm
Thou lappe me warm,
　And dance me now full oft;
And if I weep
And will not sleep,
　Then sing 'by, by, lully, lulley.'"

"Jesu, my son, heaven king,
If it be thy will,
Grant thou thee mine asking,
As reason would, and skill;
What so ever they be
That can and will be
　Merry on this day,
To bliss them bring,
And I shall sing:
　'Lulley, by, by, lully, lulley.'"

Anon

PURITAN OBJECTIONS TO CHRISTMAS

From William Prynne's "Histrio-Mastix"

OUR Christmas lords of Misrule, together with dancing, masques, mummeries, stage-players, and such other Christmas disorders, now in use with Christians, were derived from these Roman Saturnalia and Bacchanalian festivals; which should cause all pious Christians eternally to abominate them.

From "Canterbury Christmas: or A True Relation of the Insurrection at Canterbury"

UPON Wednesday, Decem. 22, the Cryer of Canterbury by the appointment of Master Major [i.e., Mayor] openly proclaimed that Christmas day, and all other Superstitious Festivals should be put downe, and that a Market should be kept upon Christmas day. Which not being observed (but very ill taken by the Country) the towne was thereby unserved with provision, and trading very much hindered; which occasioned great discontent among the people, causing them to rise in a Rebellious way.

The Major being slighted, and his Commands observed only of a few who opened their Shops, to the number of 12 at the most: They were commanded by the multitude to shut up again, but refusing to obey, their ware was thrown up and down, and they, at last, forced to shut in.

The Major and his assistants used their best endeavours to qualifie this tumult, but the fire being once kindled, was not easily quenched. The Sheriffe laying hold of a fellow, was stoutly resisted; which the Major perceiving, took a Cudgell and strook the man; who, being no puny, pulled up his courage, and knockt down the Major, whereby his Cloak was much torne and durty, beside the hurt he received. The Major thereupon made strict Proclamation for keeping the Peace and that every man depart to his own house. The multitude hollowing thereat, in disorderly manner; the Aldermen and Constables caught two or three of the rout, and sent them to Jayle, but they soon broke loose, and jeered Master Alderman.

Soone after, issued forth the Commanders of this Rabble, with an addition of Souldiers, into the high street, and brought with them two Foot-balls, whereby their company increased. Which the Major and Aldermen perceiving, took what prisoners they had got, and would have carried them to the Jayle. But the multitude following after to the King's Bench, were opposed by Captain Bridg, who was straight knoct down, and had his head broke in two places, not being able to withstand the multitude, who, getting betwixt him and the Jayle, rescued their fellowes, and beat the Major and Aldermen into their houses, and then cried Conquest.

From "The Flying Eagle", 24th December 1652

THE House spent much Time this Day about the business of the Navie, for settling the Affairs at Sea, and before they rose, were presented with a terrible Remonstrance against Christmas day, grounded upon divine Scriptures: 2 Cor. v. 16; 1 Cor. xv. 14, 17; and in humour of the Lord's day, grounded on these Scriptures: John xx. 1; Rev. i.10; Psalms cxviii. 24; Lev. xxiii. 7, 11; Mark xv. 8; Psalms lxxxiv. 10; in which Christmas is called Anti-Christ's-masse, and those Massemongers and Papists who observe it, etc.

In consequence of which, Parliament spent some time in Consultation about the Abolition of Christmas-day, pass'd Orders to that Effect, and resolv'd to sit on the following day, which was commonly called Christmas-day.

From John Evelyn's "Diary"

25th Dec., 1652 Christmas-day, no sermon any where, no church being permitted to open, so observed it at home. The next day, we went to Lewisham, where an honest divine preached.

25th Dec., 1654 Christmas-day. No public offices in churches, but penalties on observers, so I was constrained to celebrate it at home.

25th Dec., 1655 There was no more notice taken of Christmas-day in churches. I went to London, where Dr Wild preached the funeral sermon of Preaching, this being the last day; after which, Cromwell's proclamation was to take place, that none of the Church of England should dare either to preach, or administer Sacraments, teach schools, etc., on pain of imprisonment, or exile. So this was the mournfulest day that my life had seen, or the Church of England herself, since the Reformation; to the great rejoicing of both Papist and Presbyter. So pathetic was his discourse, that it drew many tears from the auditory. Myself, wife, and some of our family, received the Communion; God make me thankful, who hath hitherto provided for us the food of our souls as well as bodies! The Lord Jesus pity our distressed Church, and bring back the captivity of Zion!

25th Dec., 1657 I went to London with my wife, to celebrate Christmas-day, Mr Gunning preaching in Exeter chapel, on Micah vii, 2. Sermon ended, as he was giving us the Holy Sacrament, the chapel was surrounded with soldiers, and all the communicants and assembly surprised and kept prisoners by them, some in the house, others carried away. It fell to my share to be confined to a room in the house, where yet I was permitted to dine with the master of it, the Countess of Dorset, Lady Hatton, and some others of quality who invited me. In the afternoon came Colonel Whalley, Goffe, and others, from Whitehall to examine us one by one; some they committed to the Marshal, some to prison. When I came before them, they took my name and abode, examined me why, contrary to the ordinance made, that none should any longer observe the superstitious time of the Nativity (so esteemed by them), I durst offend, and particularly be at Common Prayers, which they told me was but the mass in English, and particularly pray for Charles Stuart; for which we had no scripture. I told them we did not pray for Charles Stuart, but for all Christian Kings, Princes, and Governors. They replied, in so doing we prayed for the King of Spain, too, who was their enemy and a Papist, with other frivolous and ensnaring questions, and much threatening; and, finding no colour to detain me, they dismissed me with much pity of my ignorance. These were men of high flight and above ordinances, and spake spiteful things of our Lord's Nativity. As we went up to receive the Sacrament, the miscreants held their muskets against us, as if they would have shot us at the altar, but yet suffering us to finish the office of Communion, as perhaps not having instructions what to do, in case they found us in that action. So I got home late the next day, blessed be God!

25th Dec., 1658 Here was no public service, but what was privately used.

THE GLASTONBURY THORN

From John Aubrey's "Memoires of Remarques in Wilts."

MR Anthony Hinton, one of the officers of the Earle of Pembroke, did inoculate, not long before the late civill warres (ten yeares or more), a bud of Glastonbury Thorne, on a thorne, at his farmhouse, at Wilton, which blossoms at Christmas, as the other did. My mother has had branches of them for a flowerpott, several Christmasses, which I have seen. Elias Ashmole, Esq., in his notes upon *Theatrum Chymicum*, saies that in the churchyard of Glastonbury grew a walnut tree that did putt out young leaves at Christmas, as doth the King's Oak in the New Forest. In Parham Park, in Suffolk (Mr Boutele's), is a pretty ancient thorne, that blossoms like that at Glastonbury, the people flock hither to see it on Christmas Day. But in the rode that leades from Worcester to Droitwiche is a black thorne hedge at Clayes, half a mile long or more, that blossoms about Christmas Day, for a week or more together. Dr Ezerel Tong sayd that about Rumly-Marsh, in Kent, are Thornes naturally like that near Glastonbury. The soldiers did cutt downe that near Glastonbury; the stump remaines.

From "*The Gentleman's Magazine,* 1753

Quainton in Buckinghamshire, December 24, 1752. Above 2,000 people came here this night, with lanthorns and candles, to view a black thorn which grows in the neighbourhood, and which was remembered (this year only) to be a slip from the famous Glastonbury Thorne, that it always budded on the 24th, was full blown the next day, and went all off at night; but the people, finding no appearance of a bud, 'twas agreed by all, that 25 December, N.S., could not be the right Christmas Day, and accordingly, refused going to Church and treating their friends on that day, as usual; at length the affair became so serious that the ministers of the neighbouring villages, in order to appease the people, thought it prudent to give notice that the old Christmas Day should be kept holy as before.

Glastonbury. A vast concourse of people attended the noted thorns on Christmas Eve, New Stile; but, to their great disappointment, there was no appearance of its blowing, which made them watch it narrowly the 5th of Jan., the Christmas Day, Old Style, when it blow'd as usual.

From Dylan Thomas' "Quite Early One Morning"

MEMORIES OF CHRISTMAS

ONE Christmas was so much like another, in those years, around the sea corner now, and out of all sound except the distant speaking of the voices I sometimes hear a moment before sleep, that I can never remember whether it snowed for six days and six nights when I was twelve or whether it snowed for twelve days and twelve nights when I was six; or whether the ice broke and the skating grocer vanished like a snowman through a white trap-door on that same Christmas Day that the mince-pies finished Uncle Arnold and we tobogganed down the seaward hill, all the afternoon, on the best tea-tray, and Mrs Griffiths complained, and we threw a snowball at her niece, and my hands burned me so, with the heat and the cold, when I held them in front of the fire, that I cried for twenty minutes and then had some jelly.

All the Christmases roll down the hill towards the Welsh-speaking sea, like a snowball growing whiter and bigger and rounder, like a cold and headlong moon bundling down the sky that was our street; and they stop at the rim of the ice-edged, fish-freezing waves, and I plunge my hands in the snow and bring out whatever I can find; holly or robins or pudding, squabbles and carols and oranges and tin whistles, and the fire in the front room, and bang go the crackers, and holy, holy, holy, ring the bells, and the glass bells shaking on the tree, and Mother Goose, and Struwelpeter—oh! the baby-burning flames and the clacking scissormen!— Billy Bunter and Black Beauty, Little Women and boys who have three helpings, Alice and Mrs Potter's badgers, penknives, teddy-bears—named after a Mr Theodore Bear, their inventor, or father, who died recently in the United States— mouth-organs, tin-soldiers, and blancmange, and Aunt Bessie playing "Pop Goes the Weasel" and "Nuts in May" and "Oranges and Lemons" on the untuned piano in the parlour all through the thimble-hiding musical-chairing blind-man's buffing party at the end of the never-to-be-forgotten day at the end of the un-remembered year.

Now out of that bright white snowball of Christmas gone comes the stocking, the stocking of stockings, that hung at the foot of the bed with the arm of a golliwog dangling over the top and small bells ringing in the toes. There was a company, gallant and scarlet but never nice to taste though I always tried when very young, of belted and busbied and musketed lead soldiers so soon to lose their heads and legs in the wars on the kitchen table after the tea-things, the mince-pies, and the cakes that I helped to make by stoning the raisins and eating them, had been cleared away; and a bag of moist and many-coloured jelly babies and a folded flag and a false nose and a tram-conductor's cap and a machine that punched tickets and rang

a bell; never a catapult; once, by a mistake that no one could explain, a little hatchet; and a rubber buffalo, or it may have been a horse, with a yellow head and haphazard legs; and a celluloid duck that made, when you pressed it, a most unducklike noise, a mewing moo that an ambitious cat might make who wishes to be a cow; and a painting-book in which I could make the grass, the trees, the sea, and the animals any colour I pleased: and still the dazzling sky-blue sheep are grazing in the red field under a flight of rainbow-beaked and pea-green birds.

Christmas morning was always over before you could say Jack Frost. And look! suddenly the pudding was burning! Bang the gong and call the fire-brigade and the book-loving firemen! Someone found the silver threepenny-bit with a currant on it; and the someone was always Uncle Arnold. The motto in my cracker read:

Let's all have fun this Christmas Day
Let's play and sing and shout hooray!

and the grown-ups turned their eyes towards the ceiling, and Auntie Bessie, who had already been frightened, twice, by a clockwork mouse, whimpered at the sideboard and had some elderberry wine. And someone put a glass bowl full of nuts on the littered table, and my uncle said, as he said once every year: "I've got a shoe-nut here. Fetch me a shoe-horn to open it, boy."

And dinner was ended.

FINE OLD CHRISTMAS

From George Eliot's "The Mill on the Floss"

FINE old Christmas, with the snowy hair and ruddy face, had done his duty that year in the noblest fashion, and had set off his rich gifts of warmth and colour with all the heightening contrast of frost and snow.

Snow lay on the croft and river-bank in undulations softer than the limbs of infancy; it lay with the neatliest finished border of every sloping roof, making the dark-red gables stand out with a new depth of colour; it weighed heavily on the laurels and fir-trees, till it fell from them with a shuddering sound; it clothed the rough turnip-field with whiteness, and made the sheep look like dark blotches; the gates were all blocked up with the sloping drifts, and here and there a disregarded four-footed beast stood as if petrified "in unrecumbent sadness"; there was no gleam, no shadow, for the heavens, too, were one still, pale cloud—no sound or motion in anything but the dark river that flowed and moaned like an unresting sorrow. But old Christmas smiled as he laid this cruel-seeming spell on the out-door world, for he meant to light up home with a new brightness, to deepen all the richness of in-door colour, and give a keener edge of delight to warm fragrance of food; he meant to prepare a sweet imprisonment that would strengthen the primitive fellowship of kindred, and make the sunshine of familiar human faces as welcome as the hidden day-star. His kindness fell but hardly on the homeless—fell but hardly on the homes where the hearth was not very warm, and where the food had little fragrance; where the human faces had no sunshine in them, but rather the laden, blank-eyed gaze of unexpectant want. But the fine old season meant well; and if he has not learnt the secret of how to bless men impartially, it is because his father Time, with ever-unrelenting purpose, still hides that secret in his own mighty, slow-beating heart.

From Edmund Gosse's "Father and Son"

CHRISTMAS AND CONSCIENCE

ON the subject of all feasts of the Church my Father held views of an almost grotesque peculiarity. He looked upon each of them as nugatory and worthless, but the keeping of Christmas appeared to him by far the most hateful, and nothing less than an act of idolatory. "The very word is Popish," he used to exclaim, "Christ's Mass!" pursing his lips with the gesture of one who tastes asafoetida by accident. Then he would adduce the antiquity of the so-called feast, adapted from horrible heathen rites, and itself a soiled relic of the abominable Yule-Tide. He would denounce the horrors of Christmas until it almost made me blush to look at a holly berry.

On Christmas Day of this year 1857 our villa saw a very unusual sight. My Father had given strictest charge that no difference whatever was to be made in our meals on that day; the dinner was to be neither more copious than usual nor less so. He was obeyed, but the servants, secretly rebellious, made a small plum-pudding for themselves. (I discovered afterwards, with pain, that Miss Marks received a slice of it in her boudoir.) Early in the afternoon, the maids—of whom we were now advanced to keeping two—kindly remarked that "the poor dear child ought to have a bit, anyhow", and wheedled me into the kitchen, where I ate a slice of plum pudding. Shortly I began to feel that pain inside which in my frail state was inevitable, and my conscience smote me violently. At length I could bear my spiritual anguish no longer, and bursting into the study called out: "Oh! Papa, Papa, I have eaten of flesh offered to idols!" It took some time, between my sobs, to explain what had happened. Then my Father sternly said: "Where is the accursed thing?" I explained that as much as was left of it was still on the kitchen table. He took me by the hand, and ran with me into the midst of the startled servants, seized what remained of the pudding, and with the plate in one hand and me still tight in the other, ran till we reached the dust-heap, when he flung the idolatrous confectionery on to the middle of the ashes, and then raked it deep down into the mass. The suddenness, the violence, the velocity of this extraordinary act made an impression on my memory which nothing will ever efface.

From Louisa M. Alcott's "Little Women"

THE CHRISTMAS PLAY

ON Christmas night a dozen girls piled on to the bed, which was the dress circle, and sat before the blue and yellow chintz curtains in a most flattering state of expectancy. There was a good deal of rustling and whispering behind the curtain, a trifle of lamp-smoke, and an occasional giggle from Amy, who was apt to get hysterical in the excitement of the moment. Presently a bell sounded, the curtains flew apart, and the Operatic Tragedy began.

"A gloomy wood", according to the one play-bill, was represented by a few shrubs in pots, green baize on the floor, and a cave in the distance. This cave was made with a clothes-horse for a roof, bureaus for walls; and in it was a small

furnace in full blast, with a black pot on it and an old witch bending over it. The stage was dark, and the glow of the furnace had a fine effect, especially as real steam issued from the kettle when the witch took off the cover. A moment was allowed for the first thrill to subside; then Hugo, the villain, stalked in with a sword at his side, a slouched hat, black beard, mysterious cloak and boots.

After pacing to and fro in much agitation, he struck his forehead, and burst out in a wild strain, singing of his hatred of Roderigo, his love for Zara, and his pleasing resolution to kill the one and win the other. The gruff tones of Hugo's voice, with an occasional shout when his feelings overcame him, were very impressive, and the audience applauded the moment he paused for breath. Bowing with the air of one accustomed to public praise, he stole to the cavern, and ordered Hagar to come forth with a commanding, "What ho! minion! I need thee!"

Out came Meg, with grey horse-hair hanging about her face, a red and black robe, a staff, and cabalistic signs upon her cloak. Hugo demanded a potion to make Zara adore him, and one to destroy Roderigo. Hagar, in fine dramatic melody, promised both, and proceeded to call up the spirit who would bring the love philtre—

> "Hither, hither, from thy home,
>   Airy sprite, I bid thee come!
>   Born of roses, fed on dew,
>   Charms and potions canst thou brew?
>
> "Bring me here, with elfin speed,
>   The fragrant philtre which I need;
>   Make it sweet and swift and strong.
>   Spirit, answer now my song!"

A soft strain of music sounded, and then at the back of the cave appeared a little figure in cloudy white, with glittering wings, golden hair, and a garland of roses on its head. Waving a wand, it sang –

> "Hither I come,
>   From my airy home,
>   Afar in the silver moon.
>   Take this magic spell,
>   And use it well,
>   Or its power will vanish soon!"

And, dropping a small, gilded bottle at the witch's feet, the spirit vanished. Another chant from Hagar produced another apparition, not a lovely one; for with a bang an ugly black imp appeared, and, having croaked a reply, tossed a dark bottle at Hugo, and disappeared with a mocking laugh. Having warbled his thanks and put the potions in his boots, Hugo departed; and Hagar informed the audience that, as he had killed a few of her friends in times past, she has cursed him, and intends to thwart his plans and be revenged on him. Then the curtain fell, and the audience reposed and ate candy while discussing the merits of the play.

A good deal of hammering went on before the curtain rose again; but when it became evident what a master-piece of stage-carpentering had been got up no one murmured at the delay. It was truly superb! A tower rose to the ceiling; half-way up appeared a window, with a lamp burning at it, and behind the white curtain appeared Zara in a lovely blue and silver dress, waiting for Roderigo. He came in gorgeous array, with plumed cap, red cloak, chestnut love-locks, a guitar, and the boots, of course.

Kneeling at the foot of the tower, he sang a serenade in melting tones. Zara replied, and, after a musical dialogue, consented to fly. Then came the grand effect of the play. Roderigo produced a rope ladder, with five steps to it, threw one end up, and invited Zara to descend. Timidly she crept from her lattice, put her hand on Roderigo's shoulder, and was about to leap gracefully down when (Alas! alas for Zara) she forgot her train—it caught in the window—the tower tottered, leant forward, fell with a crash, and buried the unhappy lovers in the ruins!

A universal shriek arose as the russet boots waved wildly from the wreck, and a golden head emerged, exclaiming, "I told you so! I told you so!" With wonderful presence of mind, Don Pedro, the cruel sire, rushed in, dragged out his daughter with a hasty aside—"Don't laugh! Act as if it was all right!"—and, ordering Roderigo up, banished him from the kingdom with wrath and scorn.

Though decidely shaken by the fall of the tower upon him, Roderigo defied the old gentleman, and refused to stir. This dauntless example fired Zara; she also defied her sire, and he ordered them both to the deepest dungeons of his castle. A stout little retainer came in with chains, and led them away, looking very much frightened and evidently forgetting the speech he ought to have made.

Act 3 was the castle hall; and here Hagar appeared, having come to free the lovers and finish Hugo. She hears him coming, and hides; sees him put the potions into two cups of wine and bid the timid little servant: "Bear them to the captives in their cells, and tell them I shall come anon." The servant takes Hugo aside to tell him something, and Hagar changes the cups for two others which are harmless. Ferdinando, the minion, carries them away, and Hagar puts back the cup which holds the poison meant for Roderigo.

Hugo, getting thirsty after a long warble, drinks it, loses his wits, and, after a good deal of clutching and stamping, falls flat and dies; while Hagar informs him what she has done in a song of exquisite power and melody.

This was a truly thrilling scene, though some persons might have thought that the sudden tumbling down of a quantity of long hair rather marred the effect of the villain's death. He was called before the curtain, and with great propriety appeared leading Hagar, whose singing was considered more wonderful than all the rest of the performance put together.

Act 4 displayed the despairing Roderigo on the point of stabbing himself because he has been told that Zara has deserted him. Just as the dagger is at his heart a lovely song is sung under his window, informing him that Zara is true, but in danger, and he can save her if he will. A key is thrown in, which unlocks the door, and in a spasm of rapture he tears off his chains and rushes away to find and rescue his lady-love.

Act 5 opened with a stormy scene between Zara and Don Pedro. He wishes her to go into a convent, but she won't hear of it; and, after a touching appeal, is about to faint, when Roderigo dashes in and demands her hand. Don Pedro refuses, because he is not rich. They shout and gesticulate tremendously, but cannot agree, and Roderigo is about to bear away the exhausted Zara when the timid servant enters with a letter and a bag from Hagar, who has mysteriously disappeared.

The latter informs the party that she bequeaths untold wealth to the young pair, and an awful doom to Don Pedro if he doesn't make them happy. The bag is opened, and several quarts of tin money shower down upon the stage, till it is quite glorified with the glitter. This entirely softens the "stern sire": he consents without a murmur. All join in a joyful chorus, and the curtain falls upon the lovers kneeling to receive Don Pedro's blessing in attitudes of the most romantic grace.

Tumultuous applause followed, but received an unexpected check, for the cot-bed on which the "dress-circle" was built suddenly shut up and extinguished the enthusiastic audience. Roderigo and Don Pedro flew to the rescue, and all were taken out unhurt, though many were speechless with laughter. The excitement had hardly subsided when Hannah appeared, with "Mrs March's compliments, and would the ladies walk down to supper?"

THE MISTLETOE BOUGH

The mistletoe hung in the castle hall,
The holly branch shone on the old oak wall,
And the Baron's retainers were blithe and gay,
And keeping their Christmas holiday.
The Baron beheld with a father's pride
His beautiful child, young Lovel's bride,
While she with her bright eyes, seem'd to be
  The star of the goodly company.
    Oh, the mistletoe bough!
    Oh, the mistletoe bough!

"I'm wearing of dancing, now," she cried,
"Here tarry a moment; I'll hide, I'll hide.
And Lovel, be sure thou'rt the first to trace
The clue to my secret lurking place."
Away she ran, and her friends began
Each tower to search and each nook to scan,
And young Lovel cried: "Oh, where dost thou hide?
I'm lonesome without thee, my own dear bride."

They sought her that night and they sought her next day,
And they sought her in vain till a week pass'd away.
In the highest, the lowest, the loneliest spot,
Young Lovel sought wildly but found her not.
And years flew by, and their grief at last
Was cold as a sorrowful tale long past,
And when Lovel appear'd the children cried,
    "See, the old man weeps for his fairy bride!"

At length an oak chest that had long lain hid
Was found in the castle; they rais'd the lid;
And a skeleton form lay mould'ring there
In the bridal wreath of the lady fair.
Oh, sad was her fate! In sportive jest
She hid from her lord in the old oak chest.
It closed with a spring, and her bridal bloom
Lay withering there in a living tomb.

Thomas Haynes Bayly

PRINCE, FOR YOUR COMING

Prince, for your coming we had made
This night where only you might wander unafraid,
A darkness of the heart and mind
Which we, like children, had designed
To terrify the peace of our eternity.
　　Like children, too, we had deceived each other
With our fears, and mourned the loss of our serenity
　　With helpless words, and prayers to a departed Father.
In this confusion, with our own destructions
Brought near to death, the nightmare's realizations,
　　There was none to turn to. But in our own
Misguided hearts the truth, like wakening, remained
　　To rouse us from the falsehood that had grown
Beyond the game we meant, the revelation we had planned.
So in all men's hearts, lost children that we are,
The seed of sense and reason lingers, a great star
Eclipsed by the midnight of our present fears,
But that in the daylight of our faith, a paradox, appears.

James Kirkup

JOSEPH

If the stars fell; night's nameless dreams
    Of bliss and blasphemy came true,
If skies were green and snow were gold,
    And you loved me as I love you;

O long light hands and curled brown hair,
    And eyes where sits a naked soul;
Dare I even then draw near and burn
    My fingers in the aureole?

Yes, in the one wise foolish hour
    God gives this strange strength to a man.
He can demand, though not deserve,
    Where ask he cannot, seize he can.

But once the blood's wild wedding o'er,
    Were not dread his, half dark desire,
To see the Christ-child in the cot,
    The Virgin Mary by the fire?

G. K. Chesterton

NEW PRINCE, NEW POMP

Behold, a seely[1] tender babe
   In freezing winter night
In homely manger trembling lies—
   Alas, a piteous sight !

The inns are full, no man will yield
   This little pilgrim bed,
But forced he is with seely beasts
   In crib to shroud his head.

Despise him not for lying there ;
   First, what he is enquire.
An orient pearl is often found
   In depth of dirty mire.

Weigh not his crib, his wooden dish,
   Nor beast that by him feed ;
Weigh not his mother's poor attire
   Nor Joseph's simple weed.

This stable is a prince's court,
   This crib his chair of state,
The beasts are parcel of his pomp,
   The wooden dish his plate.

The persons in that poor attire
   His royal liveries wear ;
The prince himself is come from heaven—
   This pomp is prized there.

With joy approach, O Christian wight ;
   Do homage to thy king ;
And highly prize his humble pomp,
   Which he from heaven doth bring.

Robert Southwell

[1] simple, innocent, defenceless

From Edward Hall's "Chronicle"

CHRISTMAS AT GREENWICH, 1512

IN this yeare the king kept his Christmasse at Greenwich, where was such abundance of viands served to all comers of anie honest behaviour, as hath beene few times seene. And against New Yeeres night was made in the hall a castell, gates, towers, and dungeon, garnished with artillerie and weapon, after the most warlike fashion: and on the front of the castell was written *Le fortresse dangereux*, and, within the castell were six ladies cloathed in russet satin, laid all over with leaves of gold, and everie one knit with laces of blew silke and gold. On their heads, coifs and caps all of gold. After this castell had been caried about the hall, and the queene had beheld it, in came the king with five other, apparelled in coats, the one halfe of russet satin, the other halfe of rich cloth of gold; on their heads caps of russet satin embroidered with works of fine gold bullion.

These six assaulted the castell. The ladies seeing them so lustie and courageous, were content to solace with them, and upon further communication to yeeld the castell, and so they came downe and dansed a long space. And after, the ladies led the knights into the castell, and then the castell suddenlie vanished out of their sights. On the daie of the Epiphanie at night, the king, with eleven other, were disguised, after the manner of Italie; called a maske, a thing not seene before, in England; they were apparelled in garments long and broad, wrought all with gold, with visors and caps of gold. And, after the banket done, these maskers came in, with six gentlemen disguised in silke, bearing staffe torches, and desired the ladies to danse: some were content, and some refused. And, after they had dansed, and communed together, as the fashion of the maske is, they tooke their leave and departed, and so did the queene and all the ladies.

Olwen Hedley

ROYAL CHRISTMASSES AT WINDSOR

THOSE who make the annals of Windsor Castle their study see the renewal of royal Christmasses there as part of a pulsating panorama.

The dawning half-light reveals Henry I holding a Christmas court in 1127. His wooden palace dated only from 1110, forty years after William the Conqueror enclosed thirteen acres of the chalk cliff with timbered earthworks. It probably formed the earliest foundations of the State Apartments, which served as the royal residence from the thirteenth century to the nineteenth.

In this cliff-top chalet, shuttered against the battery of north winds and snow, King Henry held a state festival. Prelates and nobles saluted his daughter, the Empress Matilda, as his successor in England and Normandy. A royal guest, David I of Scotland, swore fealty to her.

Every history primer records the sequel when Henry died eight years later. The image of strife invaded even this Christmas of 1127. When the Archbishop of Canterbury crowned Henry at the celebration, the Archbishop of York tried to oust him, but was roughly prevented and his cross-bearer was turned out of the chapel.

These early Christmasses create no pattern of recognizable sentiment. They are merely isolated sidelights on regal progress. When King John spent Christmas at Windsor in 1213 his prime care seems to have been the affluence of the larder. In preparation for his coming the sheriffs of the surrounding counties were ordered to provide 3000 capons, 1000 salted eels, 400 head of swine, 100 pounds of fresh almonds, 50 pounds of white bread, spices, twenty large casks of "good and new wine" for his household and four casks of the best for himself.

In 1239 the softening grace of charity creeps in. John's son, Henry III, chose his guests from among the maimed and needy. On Christmas Day he opened the great hall of the castle in the Lower Ward to poor people, whom he fed and clothed "to the glory and honour of God". In a lesser hall attached to the palace in the Upper Ward the poor were entertained on St Stephen's Day and at Epiphany, and poor clergy were feasted and clothed on St Thomas's Day, and poor boys on Innocents' Day.

This was a flickering gesture of humanity in the long drag of the centuries. Christmas was still not devoid of policy when Elizabeth I spent the festival at Windsor in 1558. She had been queen only a few weeks, and her religious temper was still in question.

A letter written by Sir William FitzWilliams, Keeper of Windsor Great Park, on December 26 related that on Christmas Day "the queene's majestie repayryd to hyr great closet with hyr nobles and ladyes, as hath ben acustomyd yn such high feasts. And so parseving a bysshope p'paring himselfe to masse all in the olde

ffowrme, she taryyd there on'till the gospelle was done; and when all the people lokyd ffor hyr to have offryde according the olde ffaccon, she with hyr nobles reeturnyd agayn ffrom the closet and the masse onto hir pryveye chambre.''

In 1648 Charles I rode into the castle out of the rain-washed twilight of a December afternoon. It was the day before Christmas Eve, but none had means or heart to be merry. The castle was the headquarters of the Parliamentary Army, and Charles came as a prisoner with no hope of escape. '' . . . the King must be lodged in the upper castle in some of the safest rooms,'' Cromwell had instructed the Governor, Colonel Christopher Whichcott.

His composure ennobled even this last desolate Christmas a month before his execution. The issue of *Perfect Occurrences* for December 29, 1648, reported: ''The King, though the cook disappointed him of mince pies and plum porridge, yet he resolved to keep Christmas; and accordingly put on his best clothes, and himself is chaplain to the gentlemen that attend him reading and expounding the scriptures to them.'' He was ''pretty merry'', and spent much time reading sermons and his precious second folio Shakespeare, in which he wrote the words *Dum spiro spero*.

Queen Charlotte in 1800 introduced local children to the excitement of a yew tree, decked with lights and gilded fruit and surrounded with gifts. George IV, who took up residence on December 9, 1828, in the new private apartments on the east front, was a genial host at a Christmas house-warming. Gas light, plate glass windows and hot and cold baths were among the innovations with which he impressed his guests.

The modern family Christmas with its complement of illuminated trees and presents was the Prince Consort's gift to the nation, and Windsor the fount of its inexhaustible springs of joy. Christmas was his favourite festival, and his biographer, Sir Theodore Martin, says that he ''clung to the kindly custom of his native country, which makes it a day for the interchange of gifts, as marks of affection and goodwill''. Queen Victoria, who always had a Christmas tree as a child, endorsed his sentiment. When they spent the first Christmas of their married life at Windsor in 1840 each set up a tree for the other, with their presents around them.

Every year the custom was renewed in the castle, with additions for the Royal Family and the court circle. The frosted branches sparkled under the lights of coloured tapers, and gingerbread favours added their rich aroma to the fragrance of the firs. A tall tree in the drawing room and three smaller ones in the dining room illumined the gilded splendours which Sir Jeffry Wyatville had designed for George IV.

English families of all classes modelled their festivities on those at Windsor. In 1865 the widowed Queen learnt with pleasure that through the royal example Christmas trees and the exchange of gifts had become generally popular.

The Prince's tact brought German and English antiquities into festive union. Royal Christmas fare maintained its hearty English tradition. The mince pies and plum pudding which Charles I had been denied were in ample evidence, and on the sideboard stood the historic boar's head, immense game pie and stupendous baron of beef. In 1852, when publication day happened to be December 25, the *Windsor and Eton Express* reported that the royal baron weighed 446 pounds and would be placed cold on a side table at the banquet that evening.

A Devon ox bred by the Prince in Windsor Great Park was still being exhibited by her Majesty's butcher. Joints of the noble beast were to ''grace the sideboards of the King of Prussia, the King of the Belgians, and the Queen of England, simultaneously on New Year's Day''. The royal Christmas continued until Twelfth Night, when the trees were lit up for the last time.

THE KING'S FIRST CHRISTMAS BROADCAST

Broadcast by King George V on 25th December 1932

Through one of the marvels of modern science I am enabled this Christmas Day to speak to all my peoples throughout the Empire. I take it as a good omen that wireless should have reached its present perfection at a time when the Empire has been linked in closer union, for it offers us immense possibilities to make that union closer still.

It may be that our future will lay upon us more than one stern test. Our past will have taught us how to meet it unshaken. For the present work to which we are all equally bound is to arrive at a reasoned tranquillity within our borders, to regain prosperity without self-seeking, and to carry with us those whom the burden of past years has disheartened or overborne.

My life's aim has been to serve as I might towards those ends. Your loyalty, your confidence in me has been my abundant reward. I speak now from my home and from my heart to you all; to men and women so cut off by the snows, the desert, or the sea that only voices out of the air can reach them; to those cut off from fuller life by blindness, sickness, or infirmity, and to those who are celebrating this day with their children and their grandchildren – to all, to each, I wish a happy Christmas. God bless you.

From E. B. Washbourne's "Reminiscences of the Siege and Commune of Paris"

PARIS BESIEGED: CHRISTMAS DAY 1870

Dec. 25th, 1870, 98th day of the Siege. Never has a sadder Christmas dawned on any city. Cold, hunger, agony, grief, and despair sit enthroned at every habitation in Paris. It is the coldest day of the season and the fuel is very short; and the Government has had to take hold of the fuel question, and the magnificent shade-trees that have for ages adorned the avenues of this city are all likely to go in the vain struggle to save France. So says the Official Journal of this morning. The sufferings of the past week exceed by far anything we have seen. There is scarcely any meat but horsemeat, and the Government is now rationing. It carries out its work with impartiality. The omnibus-horse, the cab-horse, the work-horse, and the fancy-horse, all go alike in the mournful procession to the butchery shops— the magnificent blooded steed of the Rothschilds by the side of the old plug of the cabman. Fresh beef, mutton, pork are now out of the question. A little poultry yet remains at fabulous prices. In walking the Rue St Lazare I saw a middling-sized goose and chicken for sale in a shop-window, and I had the curiosity to step in and enquire the price (rash man that I was). The price of the goose was twenty-five dollars, and the chicken seven dollars.

TO CHRIST OUR LORD

The legs of the elk punctured the snow's crust
And wolves floated lightfooted on the land
Hunting elk living or frozen;
Inside snow melted in a basin, and a woman basted
A bird spread over coals by its wings and head.

Snow had sealed the windows; candles lit
The Christmas meal. The Christmas grace chilled
The cooked bird, being long-winded and the room cold.
During the words a boy thought, is it fitting
To eat this creature killed on the wing?

He had killed it himself, climbing out
Alone on snowshoes in the Christmas dawn,
The fallen snow swirling and the snowfall gone,
Heard it scream as the gun echoed,
Watched it drop, and fished from the snow the dead.

He had not wanted to shoot. The sound
Of wings beating into the hushed air
Had stirred his love, and his fingers
Froze in his gloves, and he wondered,
Even so hungry, could he fire? Then he fired.

Now the grace praised his wicked act. At its end
The bird on the plate
Stared at his stricken appetite.
Had there been nothing to do but surrender,
To kill and to eat? He ate as he had killed, with wonder.

At night on snowshoes on the drifting field
He wondered again, for whom had love stirred?
The stars glittered on the snow and nothing answered.
Then the Swan spread her wings, cross of the cold north,
The pattern and mirror of the acts of earth.

Galway Kinnell

SAILOR'S CAROL

Lord, the snowful sky
   In this pale December
Fingers my clear eye
   Lest seeing, I remember.

Not the naked baby
   Weeping in the stable,
Nor the singing boys
   All around my table.

Not the dizzy star
   Bursting on the pane,
Nor the leopard sun
   Pawing the rain.

Only the deep garden
   Where green lilies grow,
The sailors rolling
   In the sea's blue snow.

Charles Causley

From Richard Church's "A Stroll before Dark"
CHRISTMAS IN THE INDIAN OCEAN

THE boat was small, 12,200 tons, but we had been fortunate during that winter voyage. The horrors of storm and world-wide disaster which had swept land and sea that December had been held back like the waters of the Red Sea for the Israelites. We had just sailed down that same Red Sea, breaking through its crisp mirror surface and disturbing the reflection of the hills of Sinai on the Arabia Deserta side, and the coastal mountains of Egypt to starboard, ragged and bare both in fact and reflection. Four days of this, out of sight of land once we left the Gulf of Suez and the stage-set of so much of the Old Testament.

The heat came up from the south to meet us. It was a personality, and it dominated the manners and daily habits of the ship's company. The sombre crowd blossomed into whites and swim-suits. It grew communicative, and friendships were made, lifelong, deep-rooted overnight. We were a club, we were a family, and the seventy children aboard swirled round us while we exchanged our life-stories and other confidences over the eleven o'clock cups of soup along the promenade deck, to continue the revelations at night in the saloon, or in the bar, or in odd niches on deck under the constellations and the planets, that burned so conspicuously in this different sky, like old-fashioned lanterns.

But there is nothing new in all this. It goes on still, as it went on during the British Raj in India, and hundreds of Civil Servants and their wives have recorded the nothingness of twenty days at sea, jotting down the small contacts in their diaries, and subsequently losing the diaries, and forgetting the experience. Nobody wants to read or hear about it. Travelogues are a bore, even to the confiding traveller himself, if he will only be honest about his recollections. But that Christmas at sea two years ago has haunted me. It was banal enough, perhaps, for it was composed of all the Dickensian and Washington Irving-like ingredients, compressed into small compass and imposed upon a confined community. Rumours and inklings of it began while the boat was unloading at Aden. We went ashore there, with a day to spend. I asked the way of an Englishman who had just come out of an office on the main street. He at once befriended us, and took us up in his car to the Old Town in the Crater, to show us the medieval water reservoirs, three great stone ponds, each larger than a swimming bath. They were now dry, grassed over; but even so, gave out a sense of coolness.

Aden has a reputation for being "Hell with the lid off", a kind of mineral grill where human bodies are quickly done to a turn. But it has much shade and vegetation. It even has majestic scenery. Looked down on from the heights above the Old Town it has a touch of Italian grandeur softening its Arabian harshness. One forgets the vast oil distilleries along the coast. They are dwarfed by the hills which hide the desert behind them. I found myself murmuring "Amalfi", through my anxiety that we might miss the boat. We seemed to be so remote up there, in our host's charming modern villa, sitting at tea and giving him news of England which he had not seen for over a year. He was the architect of the new town being built to house ninety thousand people, some ten miles out of Aden.

The anxiety was not needed. Travel-neurosis, to which most of us are prone, is one of the greatest energy-wasters. I set foot on board, tired out, having done nothing but stroll, and talk, and sip tea. Only a few hours ashore; and I came back to the boat as though groping my way home; emotional about it.

We lay all night in the harbour, and just before daybreak the siren moaned, waking us. We began to move, turned, and exposed ourselves to the drama of the new moon and Venus setting together. The lights of the town were fading, and the bumboats casting off from the sides of the ship, their gaudy wares catching the first hints of dawnlight, then shrinking again as we moved away. Another departure! I felt my throat tighten, as I stood watching the diminishing scene, the lights blinking down into a thin line, the hills behind rising up and treading over the town, while behind all this the sky began to catch fire, to swirl smokily, brighter and brighter, conjuring the water into life as we left the harbour, rounded the bluff, and met the risen sun. Aden was gone. There followed two days of serene monotony; down the Gulf of Aden, round eastward to the Arabian Sea, along the wedge-shaped coast of southern Arabia. It was a formidable wall, without an

observable sign of life, either vegetable or animal. Just rock. Just stone. Yet it took on a character that made it something more; something that made it both the beginning and the end of things; ossified history, and at the same time a threat. Down the coast of the early stages of the Red Sea we had seen similar mountains of barren rock, but they at least had the occasional sign of human life; villages, patches of sere green. But here—nothing! It was terrifying, or would have been so had we not been gradually moving out to sea, softening the threat, removing it several centuries further back, perhaps. But the very indifference of its removal re-constituted the threat. One word summed it up; the word "Wait!"; half uttered, and only half heard. "Wait."

But we did not wait. We plugged on, to the rhythm of the engines, over the glassy surface of the Arabian Sea, and I plagued myself trying to ascertain where these motionless waters became the Indian Ocean. Another day passed, and nothing happened, except that far to the south we saw a whale spouting. He was almost out of sight, blubber-down below the horizon. I say nothing happened, but hour by hour we were shadowed by shoals of flying fish. Shadowed is hardly appropriate, for flying fish are made of light. As they spring obliquely out of the water their anatomy shines through the transparent plastic fin and body. They glitter. Even when they plunge up out of the water to bury themselves in air, they are electric with vitality. Aboard much was happening, once we withdrew our gaze from the fascinating, crowded nothingness of the sea, and looked around the decks. The day was December 23rd and preparations were afoot, or aplank. The wide open deck at the back of the promenade was being tented in, with sailcloth and flags. This immediately enlarged it, to about the size of the floor of the Albert Hall, whereas before it had been merely a turning point for the daily health-walk, of the over-fed passengers. We had to put up with that indoor effect for the rest of the day and evening. We sat about in this concert hall subdued in mood, and lowering our voices to more confidential tones. The sentiment of Christmas had already taken possession.

So Christmas Eve found us in mid-ocean and not merely sea. Vastness predomina-ted, above, around, below. For the waters were so clear that we could stare down into the depths, giddy with the conviction that we were falling over an ever-receding cliff-top into another universe. It looked cooler than the surface world over which we were gliding. Heat competed with vastness, and during the afternoon it won. The sun itself was dissolved into its own glory. It could not be seen. But it could be felt. Its power penetrated even into the air-conditioned saloon, where the first of the seasonal feasts was served at lunchtime.

It was a northern, temperate zone meal, and it knocked the adults down. They slept the afternoon away, under the drug of light and heat; slept on deck, in the cabins, and the saloons. Only the seventy children survived. Perhaps they had been denied a meal, because of the shape of things to come. Then at four in the afternoon the ship's bell rang, and Goan boys went round banging the mealtime gongs. The sleeping ship woke, and the children, who had been half suppressed for a couple of hours, came surging up to the bows of the ship, monitored by seamen. Up above, on the promenade deck, the adults watched the scene, pleased with their handiwork in dressing up the infants in party-clothes.

There was a shout, a shrill scream of ecstasy, from the little Pied Piper crowd in their frills and ribbons. Father Christmas, in the correct beard and dressing gown, climbed aboard over the bowsprit—yes, really climbed aboard, with a huge sack on his back, and lumbered forward on a tide of infant humanity into the main saloon, where a ceiling-high pine tree stood, covered with rime. The Master of Ceremonies, a West Indian lawyer who had made himself beloved by everybody aboard during the voyage, now took charge, and there began the greatest, wildest, yet most harmonious children's party I have ever witnessed. I did not see Bob Cratchit, but I am certain I saw his creator Mr Dickens, in a gaudy waistcoat and benevolent beard, treading through the cotton-wool snow and trying on the paper hats that were to be had by the dozen. And the sack when opened and its contents distributed by Father Christmas (still bone-dry) contained exactly seventy presents for those seventy children.

Were they subdued by the vastness of the Indian Ocean, and the temperature of 98 degrees? What do you think? I even felt chilly myself.

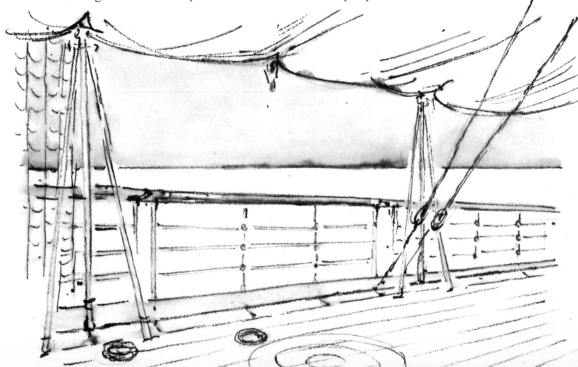

From Joseph Conrad's "Tales of Hearsay, and Last Essays"
CHRISTMAS DAY AT SEA

I N all my twenty years of wandering over the restless waters of the globe I can only remember one Christmas Day celebrated by a present given and received. It was, in my view, a proper live-sea transaction, no offering of Dead Sea fruit; and in its unexpectedness perhaps worth recording. Let me tell you first that it happened in the year 1879, long before there was any thought of wireless messages, and when an inspired person trying to prophesy broadcasting would have been regarded as a particularly offensive nuisance and probably sent to a rest-cure home. We used to call them madhouses then, in our rude, cave-man way.

The daybreak of Christmas Day in the year 1879 was fine. The sun began to shine some time about four o'clock over the sombre expanse of the Southern Ocean in latitude 51; and shortly afterwards a sail was sighted ahead. The wind was light, but a heavy swell was running. Presently I wished a "Merry Christmas" to my captain. He looked sleepy, but amiable. I reported the distant sail to him and ventured the opinion that there was something wrong with her. He said, "Wrong?" in an incredulous tone. I pointed out that she had all her upper sails furled and that she was brought to the wind, which, in that region of the world, could not be accounted for on any other theory. He took the glasses from me, directed them towards her stripped masts resembling three Swedish safety machines, flying up and down and waggling to and fro ridiculously in that heaving and austere wilderness of countless water-hills, and returned them to me without a word. He only yawned. This marked display of callousness gave me a shock. In those days I was generally inexperienced and still a comparative stranger in that particular region of the world of waters.

The captain, as is a captain's way, disappeared from the deck; and after a time our carpenter came up the poop ladder carrying an empty small wooden keg, of the sort in which certain ship's provisions are packed. I said, surprised, "What do you mean by lugging this thing up here, Chips?"—"Captain's orders, sir," he explained shortly.

I did not like to question him further, and so we only exchanged Christmas greetings and he went away. The next person to speak to me was the steward. He came running up the companion stairs: "Have you any old newspapers in your room, sir?"

We had left Sydney, N.S.W., eighteen days before. There were several old Sydney *Heralds*, *Telegraphs*, *Bulletins* in my cabin, beside a few home papers received by the last mail. "Why do you ask, steward?" I inquired naturally. "The captain would like to have them," he said.

And even then I did not understand the inwardness of these eccentricities. I was only lost in astonishment at them. It was eight o'clock before we had closed with that ship, which, under her short canvas and heading nowhere in particular, seemed to be loafing aimlessly on the very threshold of the gloomy home of storms. But long before that hour I learned from the number of boats she carried that this nonchalant ship was a whaler. She had hoisted the Stars and Stripes at her peak, and her signal flags had already told us that her name was *Alaska*—two years out from New York—east from Honolulu—two hundred and fifteen days on the cruising ground.

We passed, sailing slowly, within a hundred yards of her; and just as our steward started ringing the breakfast bell the captain and I held aloft, in good view of the figures watching us over her stern, the keg, properly headed up and containing besides an enormous bundle of newspapers, two boxes of figs in honour of the day. We flung it far out over the rail. Instantly our ship, sliding down the slope of a high swell, left it far behind in our wake. On board the *Alaska* a man in a fur cap flourished an arm; another, a much bewhiskered person, ran forward suddenly. I never saw anything so ready and so smart as the way that whaler, rolling desperately all the time, lowered one of her boats. The Southern Ocean went on tossing the two ships like a juggler his gilt balls, and the microscopic white speck of the boat seemed to come into the game instantly, as if shot out from a catapult on the enormous and lonely stage. That Yankee whaler lost not a moment in picking up her Christmas present from the English wool clipper.

Before we had increased the distance very much she dipped her ensign in thanks and asked to be reported "All well, with a catch of three fish". I suppose it paid them for two hundred and fifteen days of risk and toil, away from the sounds and sights of the inhabited world, like outcasts devoted, beyond the confines of mankind's life, to some enchanted and lonely penance.

Christmas Days at sea are of varied character, fair to middling and down to plainly atrocious. In this statement I do not include Christmas Days on board passenger ships. A passenger is, of course, a brother (or sister), and quite a nice person in a way, but his Christmas Days are, I suppose, what he wants them to be: the conventional festivities of an expensive hotel included in the price of his ticket.

From E. R. G. R. Evans' "South with Scott"

NEAR THE SOUTH POLE

CHRISTMAS Day, 1911, found our two tiny green tents pitched on the King Edward VII Plateau—the only objects that broke the monotony of the great white glittering waste that stretches from the Beardmore Glacier Head to the South Pole. A light wind was blowing from the South, and little whirls of fine snow, as fine as dust, would occasionally sweep round the tents and along the sides of the sledge runners, streaming away almost like smoke to the Northward. Inside the tents, breathing heavily, were our eight sleeping figures—in these little canvas shelters soon after 4 A.M. the sleepers became restless and occasionally one would wake, glance at one's watch, and doze again. Exactly at 5 A.M. our leader shouted "Evans" and both of us of that name replied, "Right-o, Sir."

Immediately all was bustle, we scrambled out of our sleeping-bags, only the cook remaining in each tent. The others with frantic haste filled the aluminium cookers with the gritty snow that here lay hard and windswept. The cookers filled and passed in, we gathered socks, finnesko, and puttees off the clothes line which we had rigged between the skis which were stuck upright in the snow to save them from being drifted over in the night. The indefatigable Bowers swung his thermometer in the shade until it refused to register any lower, glanced at the clouds, made a note or two in his miniature meteorological log book, and then blew on his tingling fingers, noted the direction of the wind, and ran to our tent.

Inside all had lashed up their bags and converted them into seats, the primus stove burnt with a curious low roar, and a peculiar smell of paraffin permeated the tent. By the time we had changed our footwear the savoury smell of the pemmican proclaimed that breakfast was ready. The meal was eaten with the same haste that had already made itself apparent.

A very short smoke sufficed, and Captain Scott gave the signal to strike camp. Out went everything through the little round door, down came both tents, all was packed in a jiffy on the two 12ft. sledges, each team endeavouring to be first, and in an incredibly short space of time both teams swung Southward, keeping step, and with every appearance of perfect health. But a close observer, a man trained to watch over men's health, over athletes' training, perhaps, would have seen something amiss.

The two teams, in spite of the Christmas spirit, and the "Happy Christmas" greetings they exchanged to begin with, soon lost their springy step, the sledges dragged more slowly, and we gazed ahead almost wistfully.

Yes, the strain was beginning to tell, though none of us would have confessed it. Lashly and I had already pulled a sledge of varying weight—but mostly a loaded one—over 600 miles, and all had marched this distance.

During the forenoon something was seen ahead like the tide race over a rocky ledge—it was another ice fall stretching from East to West, and it had to be crossed, there could be no more deviation, for since Atkinson's party turned we had been five points West of our course at times. Alas, more wear for the runners of the sledge, which meant more labour to the eight of us, so keen to succeed in our enterprise—soon we are in the thick of it; first one slips and is thrown violently down, then a sledge runs over the slope of a great ice wave.

The man trying to hold it back is relentlessly thrown, and the bow of the sledge crashes on to the heel of the hindmost of those hauling ahead with a thud that means "pain". But the victim utters no sound, just smiles in answer to the anxious, questioning gaze of his comrades.

Something happened in the last half of that Christmas forenoon. Lashly, whose forty-fourth birthday it was, celebrated the occasion by falling into a crevasse 8 feet wide.

Our sledge just bridged the chasm with very little to spare each end, and poor Lashly was suspended below, spinning round at the full length of his harness, with 80 feet of clear space beneath him. We had great difficulty in hauling him up on account of his being directly under the sledge. We got him to the surface by using the Alpine rope. Lashly was none the worse for his fall, and one of my party wished him a "Happy Christmas", and another "Many Happy Returns of the Day", when he had regained safety. Lashly's reply was unprintable.

Soon after this accident we topped the ice fall or ridge, and halted for lunch—
we had risen over 250 feet, according to our aneroid; it seemed funny enough to
find the barometer standing at 21 inches instead of 30.

Lunch camp, what a change. The primus stove fiercely roaring, the men light
up their pipes and talk Christmas.

After a mug of warming tea and two biscuits we strike camp, and are soon
slogging on. But the crevasses and icefalls have been overcome, the travelling is
better, and with nothing but the hard, white horizon before us, thoughts wander
away to the homeland. Next Christmas, may we hope for it?

The two teams struggled on until after 8 p.m., when at last Scott signalled to
camp. How tired we were—almost cross. But no sooner were the tents up than
eyes looked out gladly from our dirty bearded faces. Once again the cooker boiled,
and for that night we had a really good square meal—more than enough of everything—pemmican with pieces of pony meat on it, a chocolate biscuit "ragout",
raisins, caramels, ginger, cocoa, butter and a double ration of biscuits. How we
watched Bowers cook that extra thick pemmican. Had he put too much pepper
in? Would he upset it? How many pieces of pony meat would we get each? But
the careful little Bowers neither burnt nor upset the hoosh: it was up to our
wildest expectations. No one could have eaten more.

After the meal we gasped, we felt so comfortable.

But we had such yarns of home, such plans were made for next Christmas, and
after all we got down our fur sleeping-bags, and for a change we were quite warm
owing to the full amount of food which we so sorely needed.

It was unthinkable then that five out of the eight of us would soon be lying
frozen on the Great Ice Barrier, their lives forfeited by a series of crushing defeats
brought about by Nature, who alone metes out success or failure to win back for
those who venture into the heart of that ice-bound continent.

A Letter from Charles Lamb

THE ORIENTAL CHRISTMAS

To Thomas Manning (in China)   Dec. 25th., 1815

Dear Old Friend and Absentee,

This is Christmas Day 1815 with us; what it may be with you I don't know, the 12th of June next year perhaps; and if it should be the consecrated season with you, I don't see how you can keep it. You have no turkeys; you would not desecrate the festival by offering up a withered Chinese Bantam, instead of the savoury grand Norfolcian holocaust, that smokes all around my nostrils at this moment from a thousand firesides. Then what puddings have you? Where will you get holly to stick in your churches, or churches to stick your dried tea-leaves (that must be the substitute) in? What memorials you can have of the holy time, I see not. A chopped missionary or two may keep up the thin idea of Lent and the wilderness; but what standing evidence have you of the Nativity? 'Tis our rosy-cheeked, homestalled divines, whose faces shine to the tune of "Unto us a child was born", faces fragrant with the mince-pies of half a century, that alone can authenticate the cheerful mystery. I feel my bowels refreshed with the holy tide; my zeal is great against the unedified heathen. Down with the Pagodas – down with the idols—Ching-chong-fo—and his foolish priesthood! Come out of Babylon, O my friend! for her time is come; and the child that is native, and the Proselyte of her gates, shall kindle and smoke together! And in sober sense what makes you so long from among us, Manning? You must not expect to see the same England again which you left. . . .

Come as soon as you can.

           C. Lamb

From Samuel Pepys's Diary

FOUR CHRISTMAS DAYS

CHRISTMAS-DAY (1662). . . . Had a pleasant walk to Whitehall, where I intended to have received the Communion with the family, but I came a little too late. So I walked up into the house and spent my time looking over pictures, particularly the ships in King Henry the Eighth's Voyage to Bullaen; marking the great difference between those built then and now. By and by down to the chapel again, where Bishop Morley preached on the song of the angels, "Glory to God on high, on earth peace and goodwill towards men." Methought he made but a poor sermon, but long, and reprehending the common jollity of the Court for the true joy that shall and ought to be on those days. Particularized concerning their excess in plays and gaming, saying that he whose office it is to keep the gamesters in order and within bounds, serves but for a second rather in a duel, meaning the groome porter. Upon which it was worth observing how far they are come from taking the reprehensions of a bishop seriously, that they all laugh in the chapel when he reflected on their ill actions and courses. He did much press us to join in these public days of joy, and to hospitality. *But one that stood by whispered in my ears that the bishop do not spend one groate to the poor himself.* The sermon done, a good anthem followed with vialls, and the king came down to receive the sacrament.

Christmas-day (1665). To church in the morning, and there saw a wedding in the church, which I have not seen many a day; and the young people so merry one with another, and strange to see what delight we married people have to see these poor fools decoyed into our condition, every man and woman gazing and smiling at them.

Christmas-day (1667)—Being a fine, light, moonshine morning, home round the city, and stopped and dropped money at five or six places, which I was the willinger to do, it being Christmas-day, and so home, and there find my wife in bed, and Jane and the maid making pyes. So I to bed. Rose about nine, and to church, and there heard a dull sermon of Mr Mills, but a great many fine people at church; and so home. Wife and girl and I alone at dinner—a good Christmas dinner. My wife reading to me "The History of the Drummer of Dr Mompesson", which is a strange story of spies, and worth reading indeed.

Christmas-day (1668)—. . . To dinner alone with my wife, who, poor wretch! sat undressed all day till ten at night, altering and lacing of a noble petticoat; while I by her making the boy read to me the Life of Julius Caesar, and Des Cartes's book of Music.

From William Bradford's Journal
CHRISTMAS DAY WITH THE PILGRIM FATHERS, 1620

MUNDAY, ye 25 Day, we went on shore, some to fell tymber, some to saw, some to riue,[1] and some to carry, so that no man rested all that day, but towards night, some, as they were at worke, heard a noyse of some Indians, which caused us all to go to our Muskets, but we heard no further, so we came aboord againe, and left some twentie to keepe ye court of garde; that night we had a sore storme of winde and raine. Munday the 25 being Christmas day, we began to drinke water aboord, but at night, the Master caused us to have some Beere, and so on board we had diverse times now and then some Beere, but on shore none at all.

One ye day called Christmas-day, ye Gov'r caled them out to worke (as was used), but ye most of this new company excused themselves, and said it went against their consciences to worke on ye day. So ye Gov'r tould them that if they made it a mater of conscience, he would spare them till they were better informed. So he led away ye rest, and left them: but when they came home at noone from their worke, he found them in ye streets at play, openly; some pitching ye barr, and some at stoole ball, and such like sports. So he went to them and tooke away their implements, and told them it was against his conscience that they should play, and others worke. If they made ye keeping of it matter of devotion, let them kepe their houses, but there should be no gameing or revelling in ye streets. Since which time nothing hath been attempted that way, at least, openly.

[1] rive, chop

MRS DOLLY WINTHROP VISITS
SILAS MARNER

THIS good, wholesome woman could hardly fail to have her mind drawn strongly towards Silas Marner, now that he appeared in the light of a sufferer [the weaver had been robbed of his secret hoard of gold]; and one Sunday afternoon she took her little boy Aaron with her, and went to call on Silas, carrying in her hand some small lard-cakes, flat paste-like articles much esteemed in Raveloe. Aaron, an apple-cheeked youngster of seven, with a clean starched frill which looked like a plate for the apples, needed all his adventurous curiosity to embolden him against the possibility that the big-eyed weaver might do him some bodily injury; and his dubiety was much increased when, on arriving at the Stone-pits, they heard the mysterious sound of the loom.

"Ah! it is as I thought," said Mrs Winthrop sadly.

They had to knock loudly before Silas heard them; but when he did come to the door he showed no impatience, as he would once have done at a visit that had been unasked for and unexpected. Formerly, his heart had been a locked casket with its treasure inside; but now the casket was empty, and the lock was broken. Left groping in darkness, with his prop utterly gone, Silas had inevitably a sense, though a dull and half-despairing one, that if any help came to him it must come from without. . . . He opened the door wide to admit Dolly, but without otherwise returning her greeting than by moving the arm-chair a few inches as a sign that she was to sit down in it. Dolly, as soon as she was seated, removed the white cloth that covered her lard-cakes, and said in her gravest way:

"I'd a baking y'sterday, Master Marner, and the lard-cakes turned out better nor common, and I'd ha' asked you to accept some, if you thought well. I don't eat such things myself, for a bit o' bread's what I like from one year's end to the other; but men's stomichs are made so comical, they want a change, they do, God help 'em."

Dolly sighed gently as she held out the cakes to Silas, who thanked her kindly, and looked very close at them, absently. . . .

But now, little Aaron, having become used to the weaver's awful presence, had advanced to his mother's side, and Silas, seeming to notice him for the first time, tried to return Dolly's signs of goodwill by offering the lad a bit of lard-cake. Aaron shrank back a little, and rubbed his head against his mother's shoulder, but still thought the piece of cake worth the risk of putting his hand out for it.

"Oh, for shame, Aaron," said his mother, taking him on her lap, however; "why, you don't want cake again yet awhile. He's wonderful hearty," she went on, with a little sigh—"that he is, God knows. . . . "

"And he's got a voice like a bird—you wouldn't think," Dolly went on; "he can sing a Christmas carril as his father's taught him. . . . Come, Aaron, stan' up and sing the carril to Master Marner, come." . . .

Aaron was not indisposed to display his talents, even to an ogre, under protecting circumstances; and after a few more signs of coyness, consisting chiefly in rubbing the backs of his hands over his eyes, and then peeping between them at Master Marner, to see if he looked anxious for the "carril", he at length allowed his head to be duly adjusted, and standing behind the table, which let him appear above it only as far as his broad frill, so that he looked like a cherubic head untroubled with a body, he began with a clear chirp, and in a melody that had the rhythm of an industrious hammer—

> "God rest you, merry gentlemen,
> Let nothing you dismay,
> For Jesus Christ our Saviour
> Was born on Christmas-day."

Dolly listened with a devout look, glancing at Marner in some confidence that this strain would help to allure him to church.

"That's Christmas music," she said, when Aaron had ended, and had secured his piece of cake again. "There's no other music equil to the Christmas music—'Hark the erol angils sing'. And you may judge what it is at church, Master Marner, with the bassoon and the voices, as you can't help thinking you've got to a better place a'ready—for I wouldn't speak ill o' this world, seeing as Them put us in it as knows best—but what wi' the drink, and the quarrelling, and the bad illnesses, and the hard dying, as I've seen times and times, one's thankful to hear of a better. The boy sings pretty, don't he, Master Marner?"

"Yes," said Silas absently, "very pretty."

The Christmas carol, with its hammer-like rhythm, had fallen on his ears as strange music, quite unlike a hymn, and could have none of the effect Dolly contemplated. But he wanted to show her that he was grateful, and the only mode that occurred to him was to offer Aaron a bit more cake.

"Oh no, thank you, Master Marner," said Dolly, holding down Aaron's willing hands. "We must be going home now. And so I wish you goodbye, Master Marner; and if you ever feel anyways bad in your inside, as you can't fend for yourself, I'll come and clean up for you, and get you a bit of victual, and willing. But I beg and pray of you to leave off weaving of a Sunday, for it's bad for soul and body— and the money that comes i' that way 'ull be a bad bed to lie down on at the last, if it doesn't fly away, nobody knows where, like the white frost. . . ."

Silas said "Goodbye and thank you kindly", as he opened the door for Dolly, but he couldn't help feeling relieved when she was gone—relieved that he might weave again and moan at his ease. . . . The fountains of human love and faith in a divine love had not yet been unlocked, and his soul was still the shrunken rivulet, with only this difference that its little groove of sand was blocked up, and it wandered confusedly against dark obstruction.

And so, notwithstanding the honest persuasions of Mr Macey and Dolly Winthrop, Silas spent his Christmas-day in loneliness, eating his meat in sadness of heart, though the meat had come to him as a neighbourly present. In the morning he looked out on the black frost that seemed to press cruelly on every blade of grass, while the half-icy red pool shivered under the bitter wind; but towards evening the snow began to fall, and curtained from him even that dreary outlook, shutting him close up with his narrow grief. And he sat in his robbed home through the livelong evening, not caring to close his shutters or lock his door, pressing his head between his hands and moaning, till the cold grasped him and told him that his fire was grey. . . .

But in Raveloe village the bells rang merrily, and the church was fuller than all through the rest of the year, with red faces among the abundant dark-green boughs— faces prepared for a longer service than usual by an arduous breakfast of toast and ale. Those green boughs, the hymn and anthem never heard but at Christmas— even the Athanasian Creed, which was discriminated from the others only as being longer and of exceptional virtue, since it was only read on rare occasions— brought the vague exulting sense, for which the grown men could as little have found words as the children, that something great and mysterious had been done for them in heaven above and in earth below, which they were appropriating by their presence. And then the red faces made their way through the black biting frost to their own homes, feeling themselves free for the rest of the day to eat, drink, and be merry, and using that Christian freedom without diffidence.

From Sir Compton Mackenzie's "My Life and Times: Octave One"

FIVE YEARS OLD, 1888

WE went to Southport for Christmas, and Southport was without rival as a place in which to spend Christmas. Nowhere else in Great Britain was such a street as Lord Street to make one feel the spirit of Christmas. In these days of commercialized Christmas, when competition demands that every shopping street in every town shall bedeck itself, and that every big store shall have a frowsy Father Christmas hanging around from November onwards, the Lord Street of 1888 might not seem such a wonder as it seemed then. Then it was unique. Strings of fairy lamps were suspended along the length of it, and let it be remembered that fairy lamps in those days were not simultaneously lighted up by electricity. The nightlight in each one had to be lighted separately and every day the nightlights of the day before had to be taken out and replaced with new nightlights. As I write about nightlights I wonder how many contemporary readers under sixty know what I am writing about. As I remember, one could get nightlights that burned for eight or for six hours; I suppose they must have been mostly wax.

The Winter Garden was a paradise for children. I look back to it with gratitude for the delights it provided, perhaps the most cherished of all being a large bran tub into which one made lucky dips to extract treasures. The bran tub as I recall it was even better than the large Christmas tree hung with presents.

But the warmth and glow of Christmas in Southport was all too soon in the past for another long year until Christmas came again.

From Alexander Smith's "Dreamthorp"

IN SOLITARY CONTENTMENT

THIS, then, is Christmas 1862. Everything is silent in Dreamthorp. The smith's hammer reposes beside the anvil. The weaver's flying shuttle is at rest. Through the clear wintry sunshine the bells this morning rang from the gray church tower amid the leafless elms, and up the walk the villagers trooped in their best dresses and their best faces—the latter a little reddened by the sharp wind: mere redness in the middle aged; in the maids, wonderful bloom to the eyes of their lovers—and took their places decently in the ancient pews. The clerk read the beautiful prayers of our Church, which seem more beautiful at Christmas than at any other period. . . . The discourse that followed possessed no remarkable thoughts; it dealt simply with the goodness of the Maker of heaven and earth, and the shortness of time, with the duties of thankfulness and charity to the poor; and I am persuaded that every one who heard returned to his house in a better frame of mind. And so the service remitted us all to our own homes, to what roast-beef and plum-pudding slender means permitted, to gatherings around cheerful fires, to half-pleasant, half-sad remembrances of the dead and the absent.

From sermon I have returned like the others, and it is my purpose to hold Christmas alone. I have no one with me at table, and my own thoughts must be my Christmas guests. Sitting here, it is pleasant to think how much kindly feeling exists this present night in England. By imagination I can taste of every table, pledge every toast, silently join in every roar of merriment. I become a sort of universal guest. With what propriety is this jovial season placed amid dismal December rains and snows! How one pities the unhappy Australians, with whom everything is turned topsy-turvy, and who hold Christmas at midsummer! The face of Christmas glows all the brighter for the cold. The heart warms as the frost increases. Estrangements which have embittered the whole year, melt in tonight's hospitable smile. There are warmer hand-shakings on this night than during the bypast twelve months. Friend lives in the mind of friend. There is more charity at this time than at any other. You get up at midnight and toss your spare coppers to the half-benumbed musicians whistling beneath your windows, although at any other time you would consider their performance a nuisance, and call angrily for the police. Poverty, and scanty clothing, and fireless grates, come home at this season to the bosoms of the rich, and they give of their abundance. The very red-breast of the woods enjoys his Christmas feast. Good feeling incarnates itself in plum-pudding. The Master's words, "The poor ye have always with you," wear at this time a deep significance. For at least one night on each year over all Christendom there is brotherhood. And good men, sitting amongst their families, or by a solitary fire like me, when they remember the light that shone over the poor clowns huddling on the Bethlehem plains eighteen hundred years ago, the apparition of shining angels overhead, the song, "Peace on earth and goodwill toward men", which for the first time hallowed the midnight air, pray for that strain's fulfilment, that battle and strife may vex the nations no more, that not only on Christmas-eve, but the whole year round, men shall be brethren, owning one Father in heaven. . . .

Once again, for the purpose of taking away all solitariness of feeling, and of connecting myself, albeit only in fancy, with the proper gladness of the time, let me think of the comfortable family dinners now being drawn to a close, of the good wishes uttered, and the presents made, quite valueless in themselves, yet felt to be invaluable from the feelings from which they spring; of the little children, by sweetmeats lapped in Elysium; and of the pantomime, pleasantest Christmas sight of all, with the pit a sea of grinning delight, the boxes a tier of beaming juvenility, the galleries, piled up to the far-receding roof, a mass of happy laughter which a clown's joke brings down in mighty avalanches. In the pit, sober people relax themselves, and suck oranges and quaff ginger-pop; in the boxes, Miss, gazing through her curls, thinks the Fairy Prince the prettiest creature she ever beheld, and Master, that to be a clown must be the pinnacle of human happiness; while up in the galleries the hard literal world is for an hour sponged out and obliterated; the chimney-sweep forgets, in his delight when the policeman comes to grief, the harsh call of his master, and Cinderella, when the demons are foiled, and the long-parted lovers meet and embrace in a paradise of light and pink gauze, the grates that must be scrubbed tomorrow. All bands and trappings of toil are for one hour loosened by the hands of imaginative sympathy. What happiness a single theatre can contain! And those of maturer years, or of more meditative temperament, sitting at the pantomime, can extract out of the shifting scenes meanings suitable to themselves; for the pantomime is a symbol or adumbration of human life. Have we not all known Harlequin, who rules the roost, and has the pretty Columbine to himself? Do we not all know that rogue of a clown with his peculating fingers, who brazens out of every scrape, and who conquers the world by good humour and ready wit? And have we not seen Pantaloons not a few, whose fate it is to get all the kicks and lose all the halfpence, to fall through all the trap-doors, break their shins over all the burrows, and be for ever captured by the policeman, while the true pilferer, the clown, makes his escape with the booty in his possession?

Methinks I know the realities of which these things are but the shadows; have met with them in business, have sat with them at dinner. But tonight no such notions as these intrude; and when the torrent of fun, and transformation, and practical joking which rushed out of the beautiful fairy world, is in the beautiful fairy world gathered up again, the high-heaped happiness of the theatre will disperse itself, and the Christmas pantomime will be a pleasant memory the whole year through. Thousands on thousands of people are having their midriffs tickled at this moment; in fancy I see their lighted faces, in memory I hear their mirth.

By this time I should think every Christmas dinner at Dreamthorp or elsewhere has come to an end. Even now in the great cities the theatres will be dispersing. The clown has wiped the paint off his face. Harlequin had laid aside his wand, and divested himself of his glittering raiment; Pantaloon, after refreshing himself with a pint of porter, is rubbing his aching joints; and Columbine, wrapped up in a shawl, and with sleepy eyelids, has gone home in a cab. Soon, in the great theatre, the lights will be put out, and the empty stage will be left to ghosts. Hark! midnight from the church tower vibrates through the frosty air. I look out on the brilliant heaven, and see a milky way of powdery splendour wandering through it, and clusters and knots of stars and planets shining serenely in the blue frosty spaces; and the armed apparition of Orion, his spear pointing away into immeasurable space, gleaming overhead; and the familiar constellation of the Plough dipping down into the west; and I think when I go in again that there is one Christmas the less between me and my grave.

SPANISH CAROL

Tr. J. B. Trend

Galician
(arr. from Pedrell)

In moderate time

VOICES IN
UNISON

1. Up now, lag-gard-ly lass - es, Up, a-wake and a-way!
2. See the tears in his eyes, now; (Sleep, my pret - ty one, sleep!)

Out and gone be-fore cock - crow, On the road be-fore day!
Let him dream when he can, now; (Sleep, my in - no-cent, sleep!)

Ma - ry meek and gen - tle, Rose of Je - ri - cho,
Ah, my pre - cious jew - el, Great the grief and pain,

Bore a babe and laid him In a man - ger low.
Suf - fered through the wide world For the sins of men!

GOOD KING WENCESLAS

Piae Cantiones

J. M. Neale

Arr. Martin Shaw

SOPRANO
ALTO

TENOR
BASS

1. Good King Wen-ces - las looked out, On the Feast of Ste - phen,
2. 'Hi - ther, page, and stand by me, If thou know'st it, tell - ing,

When the snow lay round a - bout, Deep, and crisp, and ev - en:
Yon - der pea - sant, who is he? Where and what his dwell - ing?'

Bright-ly shone the moon that night, Though the frost was cru - el,
'Sire, he lives a good league hence, Un - der-neath the moun - tain,

When a poor man came in sight,—Gath'-ring win-ter fu - el.
Right a - gainst the for - est fence,— By Saint Ag - nes' foun - tain.'

3 'Bring me flesh, and bring me wine,
    Bring me pine-logs hither:
  Thou and I will see him dine,
    When we bear them thither.'
  Page and monarch, forth they went,
    Forth they went together:
  Through the rude wind's wild lament
    And the bitter weather.

4 'Sire, the night is darker now,
    And the wind blows stronger:
  Fails my heart, I know not how:
    I can go no longer.'
  'Mark my footsteps, good my page:
    Tread thou in them boldly:
  Thou shalt find the winter's rage
    Freeze thy blood less coldly.'

5 In his master's steps he trod,
    Where the snow lay dinted:
  Heat was in the very sod
    Which the saint had printed.
  Therefore, Christian men, be sure,
    Wealth or rank possessing,
  Ye who now will bless the poor,
    Shall yourselves find blessing.

O LITTLE TOWN

Bishop Phillips Brooks

English traditional
Arr. R. Vaughan Williams

1. O lit - tle town of Beth - le - hem, How
   A - bove thy deep and dream - less sleep The
2. O morn - ing stars, to - ge - ther Pro -
   And prais - es sing to God the King, And

still we see thee lie!
si - lent stars go by. (1.) Yet in thy dark streets
-claim the ho - ly birth, (2.) For Christ is born of
peace to men on earth;

shi - neth The ev - er - last - ing light; The
Ma - ry; And, gath - ered all a - bove, While

hopes and fears of all the years Are met in thee to - night.
mor - tals sleep, the an - gels keep Their watch, of wond-'ring love.

3 How silently, how silently,
     The wondrous gift is given!
  So God imparts to human hearts
     The blessings of his heaven.
  No ear may hear his coming;
     But in this world of sin,
  Where meek souls will receive him, still
     The dear Christ enters in.

4 Where children pure and happy
     Pray to the blessèd child,
  Where misery cries out to thee,
     Son of the mother mild;
  Where charity stands watching
     And faith holds wide the door,
  The dark night wakes, the glory breaks,
     And Christmas comes once more.

5 O holy child of Bethlehem,
     Descend to us, we pray;
  Cast out our sin, and enter in,
     Be born in us to-day.
  We hear the Christmas angels
     The great glad tidings tell:
  O come to us, abide with us,
     Our Lord Emmanuel.

15

WASSAIL SONG

North of England traditional

Traditional
Arr. Martin Shaw

SOPRANO SOLO

1. Here we come a-was-sail-ing A-mong the leaves so
2. *Our was-sail cup is made Of the rose-ma-ry
3. We are not dai-ly beg-gars That beg from door to
4. *Call up the but-ler of this house, Put on his gol-den

(Acct.) Here we come, we come,

In each verse the three under parts sing the same words during the solo

green, Here we come a-wan-der-ing, So fair to be seen:
tree, And so is your beer Of the best bar-ley:
door, But we are neigh-bours' chil-dren Whom you have seen be-fore:
ring; Let him bring us up a glass of beer, And bet-ter we shall sing:

Here we come, we come.

A hap-py New Year, we come, we come.

CHORUS

S.
A.

Love and joy come to you, And to you your was-sail

T.
B.

Love and joy come to

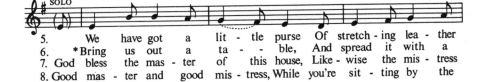

too, And God bless you, and send you A hap-py— New Year.—

you,

SOLO

5.   We have got   a   lit - tle purse Of stretch-ing lea - ther
6. *Bring us out   a   ta -   ble, And spread it with   a
7. God bless the mas - ter of   this house, Like-wise the mis - tress
8. Good mas - ter and good mis - tress, While you're sit - ting by   the

skin;— We want a lit-tle of your mo-ney To line— it well with - in:
cloth;——Bring us out— a moul-dy cheese, And some of your Christ-mas loaf:
too;—And all the lit - tle chil - dren That round— the ta - ble go:
fire,—Pray think of us poor chil-dren Who are wand -'ring in the mire:

AFTER THE FEAST

NOW FAREWELL, GOOD CHRISTMAS

Now farewell, good Christmas,
  Adieu and adieu,
I needs now must leave thee,
  And look for a new;
For till thou returnest,
  I linger in pain,
And I care not how quickly
  Thou comest again.

But ere thou departest
  I purpose to see
What merry good pastime
  This day will show me;
For a king of the wassail
  This night we must choose,
Or else the old customs
  We carelessly lose.

The wassail well spiced
  About shall go round,
Though it cost my good master
  Best part of a pound:
The maid in the buttery
  Stands ready to fill
Her nappy good liquor
  With heart and good will.

And to welcome us kindly
  Our master stands by,
And tells me in friendship
  One tooth is a-dry.
Then let us accept it
  As lovingly, friends:
And so for this twelfth-day
  My carol here ends.

                    Anon

AFTER CHRISTMAS

Gone is that errant star. The shepherds rise
And, packed in buses, go their separate ways
To bench and counter where their flocks will graze
On winter grass, no bonus of sweet hay.
The myrrh, the frankincense fade from memory:
Another year of waiting for the day.

Still in his palace Herod waits for orders;
Arrests, an edict, more judicial murders,
New taxes, reinforcements for the borders.
Still high priests preach decorum, rebels rage
At Caesar battening on their heritage
And a few prophets mourn a godless age.

The Magi in three chauffeur-driven cars
Begin their homeward journey round the wars,
Each to his capital, the stocks and shares,
Whose constellations, flickering into place,
Must guide him through a vaster wilderness
Than did the star absconded out of space.

The golden thread winds back upon the spool.
A bird's dry carcass and an empty bottle
Beside the dustbin, vomit of goodwill,
Pale streets, pale faces and a paler sky;
A paper Bethlehem, a rootless tree
Soon to be stripped, dismembered, put away,

Burnt on the grate . . . and dressed in candlelight
When next the shepherds turn their flocks about,
The three wise kings recall their second state
And from the smaller circle of the year,
Axle and weighted hub, look high and far
To pierce their weekday heaven that hides the star.

Michael Hamburger

THE NEXT DAY AFTER CHRISTMAS

The next day after Christmas, the house still hung
With streamers and gaudy paper-chains and the floor strewn
With already dying needles from the desolate tree;
The snow outside that fell, too late, in the night;
He grew up to his full stature in my drowsy mind
And at once, after so many festive nativities,
The wrench that was like death came, and I looked at him
Dispassionately and frightened, for the first time.

How many years had he taken to rob the room
Of the always festive tree, of its jovial warmth?
So many generations we cannot count them; but there
I found him, alone in the damp morning, brought
Level and down to earth and with a pitying smile
Creasing the thin corners of his bitter mouth.
Here was no Christ-child grown to manhood, but a Christ
Deliberately engendered out of the stuff of genius:

A man driven to death and torture by the insane
Ineluctable grinding of a diamond mind so sharp
It pierced to the core, leaving no other way out
But through final glory and power in hands split through
To eternal triumph on the terrible rack of the cross.
So he was a man all men might have known; a god
Built up with unfaltering care, polished as a banker,
Studied as a general with an eye for strategy.

He moved in the empty room but did not speak;
Only smiled; and when I raised up my eyes and looked
Away across the melting snow outside the window
He stepped out into the emptiness, leaving the tree cold
And as bare of tinsel as my heart of joy bare.
Then, in a corner in a torn heap, I saw lying
The cracker toys of the past night's revelry,
Twisted, akimbo, broken as the smashed world.

John Smith

233

Horace Walpole

A LETTER TO SIR HORACE MANN

DID you ever know a more absolute country-gentleman? Here am I come down to what you call keep my Christmas! indeed it is not in all the forms; I have stuck no laurel and holly in my windows, I eat no turkey and chine, I have no tenants to invite, I have not brought a single soul with me. The weather is excessively stormy, but has been so warm, and so entirely free from frosts the whole winter, that not only several of my honeysuckles are come out, but I have literally a blossom upon a nectarine-tree, which I believe was never seen in this climate before on the 26th of December.

Charles Lamb

A LETTER TO SOUTHEY

Dec. 27, 1798

Dear Southey,

Your friend John May has formerly made kind offers to Lloyd of serving me in the India house by the interest of his friend Sir Francis Baring. It is not likely that I shall ever put his goodness to the test on my own account, for my prospects are very comfortable. But I know a man, a young man, whom he could serve thro' the same channel, and I think would be disposed to serve if he were acquainted with his case. This poor fellow (whom I know just enough of to vouch for his strict integrity and worth) has lost two or three employments from illness, which he cannot regain; he was once insane, and from the distressful uncertainty of his livelihood has reason to apprehend a return of that malady. He has been for some time dependant on a woman whose lodger he formerly was, but who can ill afford to maintain him, and I know that on Christmas night last he actually walked about the streets all night, rather than accept of her Bed which she offer'd him, and offer'd herself to sleep in the kitchen; and that in consequence of that severe cold he is labouring under a bilious disorder, besides a depression of spirits which incapacitates him from exertion when he most needs it. For God's sake, Southey, if it does not go against you to ask favours, do it now—ask it as for me—but do not do a violence to your feelings, because he does not know of this application, and will suffer no disappointment. . . .

At all events I will thank you to write, for I am tormented with anxiety. . . .

C. Lamb

From Benjamin Robert Haydon's Autobiography
THE IMMORTAL DINNER PARTY

ON December 28th the immortal dinner party came off in my painting-room, with Jerusalem towering up behind us as a background. Wordsworth was in fine cue, and we had a glorious set-to,—on Homer, Shakespeare, Milton and Virgil. Lamb got exceedingly merry and exquisitely witty; and his fun in the midst of Wordsowrth's solemn intonations of oratory was like the sarcasm and wit of the fool in the intervals of Lear's passion. He made a speech and voted me absent, and made them drink my health. "Now," said Lamb, "you old lake poet, you rascally poet, why do you call Voltaire dull?" We all defended Wordsworth, and affirmed there was a state of mind when Voltaire would be dull. "Well," said Lamb, "here's to Voltaire—the Messiah of the French nation, and a very proper one too." . . .

In the morning of this delightful day, a gentleman, a perfect stranger, had called on me. He said he knew my friends, had an enthusiasm for Wordsworth and begged I would procure him the happiness of an introduction. He told me he was a comptroller of stamps, and often had correspondence with the poet. I thought it a liberty; but still, as he seemed a gentleman, I told him he might come.

When we retired to tea we found the comptroller. In introducing him to Wordsworth I forgot to say who he was. After a little time the comptroller looked down, looked up and said to Wordsworth, "Don't you think, sir, Milton was a great genius?" Keats looked at me, Wordsworth looked at the comptroller. Lamb, who was dozing by the fire, turned round and said, "Pray, sir, did you say Milton was a great genius?" "No, sir; I asked Mr Wordsworth if he were not."

236

"Oh," said Lamb, "then you are a silly fellow." "Charles! my dear Charles!" said Wordsworth; but Lamb, perfectly innocent of the confusion he had created, was off again by the fire.

After an awful pause the comptroller said, "Don't you think Newton a great genius?" I could not stand it any longer. Keats put his head into my books. Ritchie squeezed in a laugh. Wordsworth seemed asking himself, "Who is this?" Lamb got up, and taking a candle, said, "Sir, will you allow me to look at your phrenological development?" He then turned his back on the poor man, and at every question of the comptroller he chaunted—

> "Diddle diddle dumpling, my son John
> Went to bed with his breeches on."

The man in office, finding Wordsworth did not know who he was, said in a spasmodic and half-chuckling anticipation of assured victory, "I have had the honour of some correspondence with you, Mr Wordsworth." "With me, sir?" said Wordsworth, "not that I remember." "Don't you, sir? I am a comptroller of stamps." There was a dead silence—the comptroller evidently thinking that was enough. While we were waiting for Wordsworth's reply, Lamb sung out

> "Hey diddle diddle
> The cat and the fiddle."

"My dear Charles!" said Wordsworth,—

> "Diddle diddle dumpling, my son John,"

chaunted Lamb, and then rising, exclaimed, "Do let me have another look at that gentleman's organs." Keats and I hurried Lamb into the painting-room, shut the door and gave way to inextinguishable laughter. Monkhouse followed and tried to get Lamb away. We went back but the comptroller was irreconcilable. We soothed and smiled and asked him to supper. He stayed, though his dignity was sorely affected. However, being a good-natured man, we parted all in good-humour, and no ill-effects followed.

All the while, until Monkhouse succeeded, we could hear Lamb struggling in the painting-room and calling at intervals, "Who is that fellow? Allow me to see his organs once more."

It was indeed an immortal evening. Wordsworth's fine intonation as he quoted Milton and Virgil, Keats's eager inspired look, Lamb's quaint spark of lambent humour, so speeded the stream of conversation, that in my life I have never passed a more delightful time. All our fun was within bounds. Not a word passed that an apostle might not have listened to. It was a night worthy of the Elizabethan age, and my solemn Jerusalem flashing up by the flame of the fire, with Christ hanging over us like a vision, all made up a picture which will long glow upon—

> "that inward eye
> Which is the bliss of solitude."

Keats made Ritchie promise he would carry his *Endymion* to the great desert of Sahara and fling it in the midst.

From Berta Lawrence's "A Somerset Journal"

WASSAILING IN SOMERSET

AT Carhampton a fortnight ago (on Old Twelfth Night), they celebrated one of the most ancient country rituals, the wassailing of the apple-trees. Lights twinkled from the dark and leafless orchards, the wind that stirred the creaking branches carried the sound of men's voices to the village street as the wassailers trooped over the wet grass and disturbed the cropping sheep. In every orchard they surrounded the most ancient trees and fired their sporting guns into the old bare branches so that evil spirits might be scared away. They sent the youngest of their party up into the fork of the tree where he fixed a piece of cake that had been dipped in cider, then they emptied a bucketful of cider around the roots, a libation poured for the tree-spirit so that he may be pleased to grant a liberal crop of fruit next autumn. Afterwards the wassailers joined hands about the tree and sang the traditional Apple-wassail song:

> Old Apple Tree, Old Apple Tree,
> We be come to wassail thee,
> > To bear and to bow
> > Apples enow.
> Hats full! Caps full! Three bushel bags full!
> > Barns full!
> Apples and pears—
> And a little heap, under the stairs,
> > Hurray!

Here is another song sometimes sung at the wassailing:

> Wassail, wassail, in our town
> The cup is white but the ale is brown,
> The jug is made of the best clay.
> Come pretty old fellow and I will drink to thee.

Whichever song they choose as their serenade to "the pretty old fellow", they conclude with ringing cheers and a tossing up of hats before going back to the village to drink cider. If the night is very cold, they put ginger in their drink.

239

From Charles Lamb's "Essays of Elia"

NEW YEAR'S EVE

EVERY man hath two birthdays; two days, at least, in every year, which set him upon revolving the lapse of time, as it affects his mortal duration. The one is that which in an especial manner he termeth *his*. In the gradual desuetude of old observances, this custom of solemnizing our proper birthday hath nearly passed away, or is left to children, who reflect nothing at all about the matter, nor understand anything in it beyond cake and orange. But the birth of a New Year is of an interest too wide to be pretermitted by king or cobbler. No one ever regarded the First of January with indifference. It is that from which all date their time, and count upon what is left. It is the nativity of our common Adam.

Of all sound of all bells—(bells, the music nighest bordering upon heaven)— most solemn and touching is the peal which rings out the Old Year. I never hear it without a gathering-up of my mind to a concentration of all the images that have been diffused over the past twelvemonth; all I have done or suffered, performed or neglected—in that regretted time. I begin to know its worth, as when a person dies. It takes a personal colour; nor was it a poetical flight in a contemporary, when he exclaimed—

I saw the skirts of the departing Year.

It is no more than what in sober sadness every one of us seems to be conscious of, in that awful leave-taking. I am sure I felt it, and all felt it with me, last night; though some of my companions affected rather to manifest an exhilaration at the birth of the coming year, than any very tender regrets for the decease of its predecessor. But I am none of those who—

Welcome the coming, speed the parting guest.

I am naturally, beforehand, shy of novelties; new books, new faces, new years,— from some mental twist which makes it difficult in me to face the prospective. I

have almost ceased to hope; and am sanguine only in the prospects of other (former) years. I plunge into foregone visions and conclusions. I encounter pell-mell with past disappointments. I am armour-proof against old discouragements. I forgive, or overcome in fancy, old adversaries. I play over again *for love*, as the gamesters phrase it, games, for which I once paid so dear. I would scarce now have any of those untoward accidents and events of my life reversed. I would no more alter them than the incidents of some well-contrived novel.

From Tyrone Power's "Impressions of America"

NEW YEAR IN NEW YORK, 1834

January 1, 1834. On this day from an early hour every door in New York is open and all the good things possessed by the inmates paraded in lavish profusion. Every sort of vehicle is put in requisition. At an early hour a gentleman of whom I had a slight knowledge entered my room, accompanied by an elderly person I had never before seen, and who, on being named, excused himself for adopting such a frank mode of making my acquaintance, which he was pleased to add he much desired, and at once requested me to fall in with the custom of the day, whose privilege he had thus availed himself of, and accompany him on a visit to his family.

I was the last man on earth likely to decline an offer made in such a spirit; so entering his carriage, which was waiting, we drove to his house on Broadway, where, after being presented to a very amiable lady, his wife, and a pretty gentle-looking girl, his daughter, I partook of a sumptuous luncheon, drank a glass of champagne, and on the arrival of other visitors, made my bow, well pleased with my visit.

My host now begged me to make a few calls with him, explaining, as we drove along, the strict observance paid to this day throughout the State, and tracing the excellent custom to the early Dutch colonists. I paid several calls in company with my new friend, and at each place met a hearty welcome, when my companion suggested that I might have some compliments to make on my own account, and so leaving me, begged me to consider his carriage perfectly at my disposal. I left a card or two and made a couple of hurried visits, then returned to my hotel to think over the many beneficial effects likely to grow out of such a charitable custom which makes even the stranger sensible of the benevolent influence of this kindly day, and to wish for its continued observance.

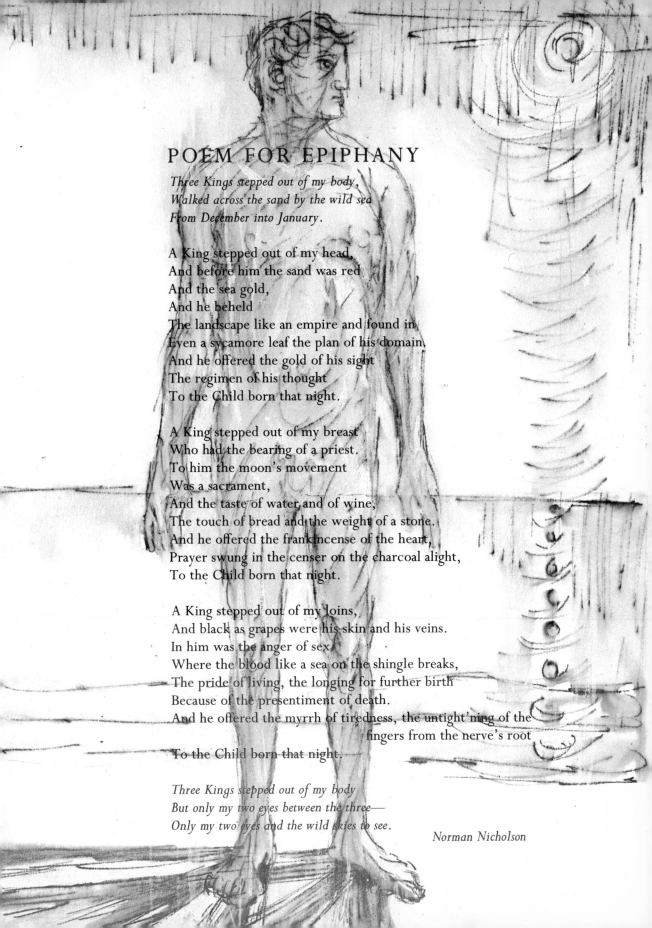

POEM FOR EPIPHANY

Three Kings stepped out of my body,
Walked across the sand by the wild sea
From December into January.

A King stepped out of my head,
And before him the sand was red
And the sea gold,
And he beheld
The landscape like an empire and found in
Even a sycamore leaf the plan of his domain.
And he offered the gold of his sight
The regimen of his thought
To the Child born that night.

A King stepped out of my breast
Who had the bearing of a priest.
To him the moon's movement
Was a sacrament,
And the taste of water and of wine,
The touch of bread and the weight of a stone.
And he offered the frankincense of the heart,
Prayer swung in the censer on the charcoal alight,
To the Child born that night.

A King stepped out of my loins,
And black as grapes were his skin and his veins.
In him was the anger of sex
Where the blood like a sea on the shingle breaks,
The pride of living, the longing for further birth
Because of the presentiment of death.
And he offered the myrrh of tiredness, the untight'ning of the
                                      fingers from the nerve's root

To the Child born that night.

Three Kings stepped out of my body
But only my two eyes between the three—
Only my two eyes and the wild skies to see.

                                      Norman Nicholson

From Charlotte Brontë's "Jane Eyre"

THE DOLL

CHRISTMAS and the New Year had been celebrated at Gateshead with the usual festive cheer; presents had been interchanged, dinners and evening parties given. From every enjoyment I was, of course, excluded: my share of the gaiety consisted of witnessing the daily apparelling of Eliza and Georgina, and seeing them descend to the drawing-room, dressed out in thin muslin frocks and scarlet sashes, with hair elaborately ringletted; and afterwards, in listening to the sound of the piano or the harp played below, to the passing to and fro of the butler and footman, to the jingling of glass and china as refreshments were handed, to the broken hum of conversation as the drawing-room door opened and closed. When tired of this occupation, I would retire from the stairhead to the solitary and silent nursery: there, though somewhat sad, I was not miserable. To speak truth, I had not the least wish to go into company, for in company I was very rarely noticed; and if Bessie had but been kind and companionable, I should have deemed it a treat to spend the evenings quietly with her, instead of passing them under the formidable eye of Mrs Reed, in a room full of ladies and gentlemen. But Bessie, as soon as she had dressed her young ladies, used to take herself off to the lively regions of the kitchen and housekeeper's room, generally bearing the candle along with her. I then sat with my doll on my knee until the fire got low, glancing round occasionally to make sure that nothing worse than myself haunted the shadowy room; and when the embers sank to a dull red, I undressed hastily, tugging at knots and strings as I best might, and sought shelter from cold and darkness in my crib. To this crib I always took my doll; human beings must love something, and, in the dearth of worthier objects of affection, I contrived to find a pleasure in loving and cherishing a faded graven image, shabby as a miniature scarecrow. It puzzles me now to remember with what absurd sincerity I doated on this little toy, half fancying it alive and capable of sensation. I could not sleep unless it was folded in my nightgown; and when it lay there safe and warm, I was comparatively happy, believing it to be happy likewise.

Long did the hours seem while I waited the departure of the company, and listened for the sound of Bessie's step on the stairs: sometimes she would come up in the interval to seek her thimble or her scissors, or perhaps to bring me something by way of supper—a bun or a cheese-cake—then she would sit on the bed while I ate it, and when I had finished, she would tuck the clothes round me, and twice she kissed me, and said, 'Good night, Miss Jane.' When thus gentle, Bessie seemed to me the best, prettiest, kindest being in the world; and I wished most intensely that she would always be so pleasant and amicable, and never push me about, or scold, or task me unreasonably, as she was too often wont to do.

From William Makepeace Thackeray's

PANTOMIMES

I often think with gratitude of the famous Mr Nelson Lee – the author of I don't know how many hundred glorious pantomimes – walking by the summer wave at Margate, or Brighton perhaps, revolving in his mind the idea of some new gorgeous spectacle of faery, which the winter shall see complete. He is like Cook at midnight *(si parva licet)*. He watches and thinks. He pounds the sparkling sugar of benevolence, the plums of fancy, the sweetmeats of fun, the figs of – well, the figs of fairy fiction, let us say, and pops the whole in the seething cauldron of Imagination, and at due course serves up the PANTOMIME.

Very few men in the course of nature can expect to see *all* the pantomimes in one season, but I hope to the end of my life I shall never forgo reading about them in that delicious sheet of *The Times* which appears on the morning after Boxing Day. Perhaps reading is even better than seeing. The best way, I think, is to say you are ill, lie in bed, and have the paper for two hours, reading all the way down from Drury Lane to the Britannia at Hoxton.

From William Hone's "Ancient Mysteries"

FEAST OF FOOLS

BELETUS, who lived in 1182, mentions the Feast of Fools, as celebrated in some places on New Year's Day, in others on Twelfth Night and in still others the week following. It seems at any rate to have been one of the recognized revels of the Christmas season. In France, at different cathedral churches there was a Bishop or an Archbishop of Fools elected, and in the churches immediately dependant upon the papal see a Pope of Fools.

These mock pontiffs had usually a proper suite of ecclesiastics, and one of their ridiculous ceremonies was to shave the Precentor of Fools upon a stage erected before the church in the presence of the jeering "vulgar populace".

They were most attired in the ridiculous dresses of pantomime players and buffoons, and so habited entered the church, and performed the ceremony accompanied by crowds of followers representing monsters or so disguised as to excite fear or laughter. During this mockery of a divine service they sang indecent songs in the choir, ate rich puddings on the corner of the altar, played at dice upon it during the celebration of a mass, incensed it with smoke from old burnt shoes, and ran leaping all over the church. The Bishop or Pope of Fools performed the service and gave benediction, dressed in pontifical robes. When it was concluded he was seated in an open carriage and drawn about the town followed by his train, who in place of carnival confetti threw filth from a cart upon the people who crowded to see the procession.

These "December liberties", as they were called, were always held at Christmas time or near it, but were not confined to one particular day, and seem to have lasted through the chief part of January. When the ceremony took place on St Stephen's Day they said as part of the Mass a burlesque composition called the Fool's Prose.

MARK WELL MY HEAVY DOLEFUL TALE

Mark well my heave doleful tale,
 For Twelfth-day now is come,
And now I must no longer sing,
 And say no words but mum;
For I perforce must take my leave
 Of all my dainty cheer,
Plum-porridge, roast beef and minced pies,
 My strong ale and my beer.

Kind-hearted Christmas, now adieu,
 For I with thee must part,
And for to take my leave of thee
 Doth grieve me at the heart;
Thou wert an ancient housekeeper,
 And mirth with meat didst keep,
But thou art going out of town,
 Which makes me for to weep.

God knoweth whether I again
 Thy merry face shall see,
Which to good-fellows and the poor
 That was so frank and free.
Thou lovedst pastime with thy heart,
 And eke good company;
Pray hold me up for fear I swoon,
 For I am like to die.

Come, butler, fill a brimmer up
 To cheer my fainting heart,
That to old Christmas I may drink
 Before he doth depart;
And let each one that's in this room
 With me likewise condole,
And for to cheer their spirits sad
 Let each one drink a bowl.

And when the same it hath gone round
   Then fall unto your cheer,
For you do know that Christmas time
   It comes but once a year.
But this good draught which I have drunk
   Hath comforted my heart,
For I was very fearful that
   My stomach would depart.

Thanks to my master and my dame
   That doth such cheer afford;
God bless them, that each Christmas they
   May furnish thus their board.
My stomach having come to me,
   I mean to have a bout,
Intending to eat most heartily;
   Good friends, I do not flout.

Anon

MAKING THE MOST OF IT

For twelve days and nights
The Christmas Tree that I bought last year
Stood unwatered and undernourished
In a flower-pot in the drawing-room.
How could we know what it felt,
Hung with coloured globes and tinsel,
Gifts and candles;
Pulled and poked about and fingered
By eager children;
Wreathed with smoke from cigars and cigarettes
And fumes of wine and punch?

When the Feast was over
I took a chance
And carefully replanted the tree in my garden,
Tenderly spreading the parched and aching roots,
Not daring to think he might live:
But he did.

Now he comes back into the house again,
Like an old servant called in for a special occasion,
Glad to be made use of,
Beaming upon the company from the serving table.

Of course I am not sure I have done the right thing.
He may catch cold, or catch warm (which is worse),
For it can't be good for trees to be dug up annually
And draped with 'frost', and tinsel,
Gleaming balls and candles,
And made to stand in sand for twelve days and nights.

We shouldn't like it if we were Christmas trees!
The only thing to do is to give him a third chance
And hope he will take it.

William Kean Seymour

ON THE TWELFTH DAY OF CHRISTMAS
I SCREAMED

(A LETTER FROM HIS GIRL TO A G.I. IN TOKYO)
Now April's here, what ever can I do
With those fantastic gifts I got from you?
Spring's in the air, but, honey, life is hard:
The three French hens are pecking in the yard,
And the turtledove, the turtledove
(One of them died)—
Ah, love, my own true love, you have denied
Me nothing the mails or the express could bring.
But look: we're into spring;
The calling birds are calling, calling;
The pear tree's leaves are slowly falling;
I sit here with those cackling geese
And never know a moment's peace.
My memories are mixed and hazy,
The drumming drummers drive me crazy,
The milking maids enjoy canasta,
The lords are leaping ever faster,
The pipers—God in Heaven knows
I've more than had enough of those.

My love, you do such wondrous things
(Who else would think of *five* gold rings?)
I know you send me all you can
Of spoils of occupied Japan,
But you remain on alien shore
And waiting here is such a bore.
My love, the lively lords are leaping:
Some things will not improve with keeping.

Now April's here, the weary days go by;
I watch that wretched dove attempt to fly;
The partridge smells; the geese are getting hoarse;
My diction's growing positively coarse
You must forgive me gestures of rejection—
I'm crazed with all your tokens of affection.
Enough's enough; next time be less romantic
And don't send gifts that drive a lady frantic.
Send me a postcard with a pretty view
And I shall look at it and think of you.

David Daiches

INDEX OF AUTHORS